THE LIFE AND ART
OF
DWIGHT WILLIAM TRYON

THE LIFE AND ART
OF
DWIGHT WILLIAM
TRYON

BY

HENRY C. WHITE

BOSTON AND NEW YORK

HOUGHTON MIFFLIN COMPANY

The Riverside Press Cambridge

1930

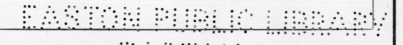

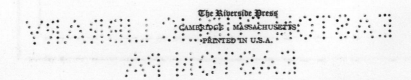

The Riverside Press
CAMBRIDGE · MASSACHUSETTS
PRINTED IN U.S.A.

TO
THE MEMORY OF
DWIGHT WILLIAM TRYON

PREFACE

Literature is not my profession. The prospect of writing a biography seems formidable, but I find that I must write one because my friend Tryon wished me to do so. 'You know me as well as any one. We have been shipmates for fifty years. I have always liked what you have written about me, and, if my life is worth recording, I think you are the one to do it.' He said this, with his characteristic directness, one morning in February about four months before his death. I had written a sketch of his life for the Smith College 'Bulletin' on the occasion of his resignation as professor of art, and Tryon was pleased with it. So on that morning in February he had come to my New York studio to thank me. It was then that the question of writing his biography arose between us.

I felt, however, that others of his friends were better equipped than I for this task, and I told him so, adding that, if he wished, I should be glad to turn over all of the material in my possession to any one he might select. To this he replied again, 'I think you are the one to do it if you will.' I accepted the task and promised him that, with due allowance for the uncertainties and vicissitudes of life, I should hope to carry out his wish;

vii

and that I should like to begin at once by obtaining from him whatever further facts I needed while he could supply them. He promised that he would begin immediately to set down, in a series of notes, a brief history of his life. This he did, writing from time to time, as his strength permitted; for he realized, as I did, that his creative work was over and that his health was failing rapidly.

In writing this book I have been very fortunate in having the generous and helpful coöperation of Mr. Tryon's friends. It is doubtful if I could have carried it to completion without their aid. Mr. Alfred Vance Churchill, long the friend and colleague of Tryon in the Art Department of Smith College, has generously given me his time in annotation and suggestion. Mr. Royal Cortissoz has kindly given me permission to quote from his excellent essay upon Tryon's art, as well as aiding me with his criticism. I have also taken advantage of an appreciation of the painter by the late Charles H. Caffin. Mr. N. E. Montross has contributed important data and recollections, and I am indebted to E. B. Dewing, the novelist, daughter of Mr. Thomas W. Dewing, for valuable criticism and collaboration. Mr. George Alfred Williams has allowed me to draw upon his interesting correspondence with Tryon on the subject of art, and Mr. Edward A. Bell, Mr. William Bailey Faxon, and Mr. Leverett Belknap have all helped to refresh my memories of the artist.

I also wish to acknowledge the courtesy shown me by the Messrs. E. and A. Milch, Mr. Robert Macbeth, and Mr. Thomas Gerrity of Knoedler & Company, who have supplied lists of pictures and given me every facility to verify dates, sales and owners.

To my son Nelson, who has been of constant help to me in the revision of my writing, I must make grateful acknowledgment.

HENRY C. WHITE

Waterford, Connecticut
June 15, 1930

CONTENTS

I. A LODGING FOR THE NIGHT   1

II. BOYHOOD   7

III. THE BOOKSTORE   15

IV. THE HARTFORD STUDIO   26

V. THE PARIS YEARS   34

VI. FOREIGN INFLUENCES   47

VII. SOUTH DARTMOUTH   58

VIII. TRYON IN NEW YORK   74

IX. THE TEACHER — SMITH COLLEGE   88

X. THE MAN   110

XI. TRYON'S FRIENDS   139

XII. TRYON'S ART   148

XIII. TECHNICAL METHODS   175

XIV. AN ARTIST'S WAY WITH THE WORLD   184

XV. RECOLLECTIONS   191

XVI. LAST DAYS   211

MEDALS AND AWARDS   217

BIBLIOGRAPHY   219

INDEX   221

ILLUSTRATIONS

DWIGHT WILLIAM TRYON. *About 1890* *Frontispiece*

HOUSE AT SOUTH DARTMOUTH 2

STUDIO, SOUTH DARTMOUTH 2

BOYHOOD HOME OF TRYON 8

CATALOGUE, WADSWORTH ATHENÆUM, 1856. 20

SCENE IN THE WHITE MOUNTAINS. *Oil, about 1872* 24
Collection of Henry C. White

CLAY CLIFFS, BLOCK ISLAND, SUNSET. *Oil, dated 1876* 28
Collection of Mr. and Mrs. Frank Bel, Hartford, Connecticut

EARLY DRAWING. *Pencil, about 1870* 32
Collection of Henry C. White

THE CNIDIAN VENUS. *Cast drawing, dated 1878, Paris* 38
Smith College Museum of Art

TRYON AND THAYER AT GUERNSEY, 1877 44
(At the left are Mr. and Mrs. Tryon, in the center beside them Mr. and Mrs.
Thayer)

THE RIVER MAAS, DORDRECHT. *Oil, 1881* 48
Smith College Museum of Art

SKETCH OF SOUTH DARTMOUTH. *Oil, 1883* 58
Smith College Museum of Art

DARTMOUTH MOORLANDS. *Oil, 1885* 62
Smith College Museum of Art

DAYBREAK, FAIRHAVEN. *Oil, 1885*   64
    Rhode Island School of Design, Providence, R.I.

NEWPORT AT NIGHT. *Oil, 1886*   66
    Collection of Burton Mansfield, Esq., New Haven, Connecticut

THE RISING MOON. *Oil, 1889*   78
    Freer Gallery of Art, Washington, D.C.
    From the wood engraving by Elbridge Kingsley

TRYON IN 1890   90

STUDY OF INTERIOR OF TRYON'S STUDIO IN REMBRANDT
BUILDING, NEW YORK, 1886   94
    From the oil painting by Henry C. White
    Collection of Henry C. White

LETTER TO MISS BEULAH STRONG   98

THE TRYON ROOM, TRYON GALLERY, SMITH COLLEGE
MUSEUM OF ART   102

INTERIOR, TRYON GALLERY, NORTHAMPTON, MASSACHU-
SETTS   102

EXTERIOR, TRYON GALLERY, NORTHAMPTON, MASSACHU-
SETTS   106

TRYON IN 1923   110

TRYON IN HIS STUDIO AT HARPERLEY HALL. *About 1920*   120

TRYON CAMPING IN CANADA, 1898   130

SLOOP 'ALICE' IN 1885   136

TRYON AT HELM OF THE 'SKAT' IN 1919   138

THE 'SKAT' IN 1919   138

AUTUMN MORNING. *Oil, 1923*   156
    Collection of Henry C. White

MORNING MIST. *Oil, October, 1922*   158
    Collection of Henry C. White

THE BROOK IN MAY. *Oil, 1902*   160
    Collection of Henry C. White

SPRINGTIME. *Oil, 1897*   164
    Freer Gallery of Art, Washington, D.C.

A NORTHEASTER. *Pastel, 1915*   168
    Freer Gallery of Art, Washington, D.C.

SUPPLEMENTARY REPRODUCTIONS OF PAINTINGS

(Following page 227)

THE PANTHEON AT NIGHT, PARIS. *Charcoal drawing, 1878*
    Smith College Museum of Art

THE WEIR, MONCHAUX. *Charcoal sketch, 1880*
    Smith College Museum of Art

PARIS, EVENING. *Crayon, 1878*
    Smith College Museum of Art

NOTRE DAME. *Oil*
    Smith College Museum of Art

CERNAY LA VILLE. *Oil, 1881*
    Smith College Museum of Art

VENICE. *Oil, 1879*
    Smith College Museum of Art

FRENCH VILLAGE, EVENING. *Charcoal, 1881*
    Smith College Museum of Art

GLASTONBURY MEADOWS. *Oil, 1881*
    Collection of W. K. Bixby, Esq., St. Louis, Missouri

EVENING, NEW BEDFORD HARBOR. *Oil, 1890*
    Metropolitan Museum of Art, New York

MOONRISE, NEAR THE SHORE. *Oil, 1887*

SELF PORTRAIT. *Oil, 1891*
    Smith College Museum of Art

EARLY SPRING. *Oil, 1894*
    Metropolitan Museum of Art, New York

SALT MARSHES, DECEMBER. *Oil, 1890*
    Smith College Museum of Art

SCENE AT NEW BEDFORD. *Oil, 1889*

DAWN. *Oil, 1906*
    Smith College Museum of Art

OCTOBER FIELDS. *Oil, 1913–14*
    Smith College Museum of Art

TWILIGHT, MAY. *Oil*
    Freer Gallery of Art, Washington, D.C.

XV

DRAWING OF TREES. *Pencil*
Collection Smith College Museum of Art

SPRINGTIME. *Oil, 1912*
Smith College Museum of Art

THE SEA BEFORE SUNRISE. *Oil, 1907*
Collection of Henry C. White

STUDY FOR A PAINTING. *Pencil, 1920*
Smith College Museum of Art

AUTUMN, NEW ENGLAND. *Oil, 1903*
Collection of W. K. Bixby, Esq., St. Louis, Missouri

NOVEMBER MORNING. *Oil, 1901–02*
Collection of John Herron, Art Institute, Indianapolis, Indiana

NOVEMBER. *Oil, 1904–05*
National Gallery of Art, Washington, D.C.

MAY MORNING. *Oil, 1906*
Collection of Henry C. White

TWILIGHT, EARLY SPRING. *Oil, 1906*
Collection of Henry C. White

NIGHT. *Pastel, 1915*
Collection of Henry C. White

EVENING, LOOKING EAST. *Pastel, 1915*
Smith College Museum of Art

OCTOBER MORNING. *Oil, 1923*
Collection of Henry C. White

NOVEMBER EVENING. *Oil, 1925*
The artist's last picture. Smith College Museum of Art

NIGHT, NEW ENGLAND. *Oil, 1906*
Collection of Dr. F. Whiting, New York

TWILIGHT SEAS. *Oil, 1907*
Freer Gallery of Art, Washington, D.C.

The illustrations are from photographs by Allison Spence, Bert Newhall, Theodosia Chase, William McKillop, and Howard G. Dine.

THE LIFE AND ART
OF
DWIGHT WILLIAM TRYON

THE LIFE AND ART OF

DWIGHT WILLIAM TRYON

I

A LODGING FOR THE NIGHT

It is fitting to approach Tryon by way of the sea. He had a dual nature. He was half artist, half sailor and fisherman. It sometimes seemed as if the sportsman predominated. It is even difficult to think of him or present him clearly outside his setting in the little village and on the waters he loved so well. Paradoxically, you found him most at home when away from home. The land was but a sea-bird's roost for him — merely a lodging for the night. A short sleep, a little food snatched on the wing, and Tryon was up and away in his boat before another sail was hoisted or the exhaust of a motor broke the stillness of the morning.

New Bedford is the nearest city to Tryon's anchorage. It has little now to remind us of the old whaling port of 1850. The great cotton mills and a mixed population whose activities are no longer maritime replace the sturdy whalers of the past. True, a few of its byways are still rough-paved, where drays loaded with casks of sperm once rumbled over the cobblestones, and at the foot of Union Street we catch a glimpse of the lone

1

hulk of a whaleship with cockbilled yards and disheveled gear.

The trolley on Purchase Street has a sign which reads, 'Padanaram.' Long usage has fixed this apocryphal name upon the village of South Dartmouth. The route of the trolley is about four miles long. Toward the end there is a little hill, and Buzzard's Bay thrusts a glittering arm into the land. It is Apponagansett Harbor, and South Dartmouth, with a long street of tall elms and old houses, hugs its eastern shore. The cool wind from the sea whips across the bay in puffs. Tryon chose his environment with unerring instinct. I doubt if he could have found a more congenial *milieu*. The happy years spent in this typical New England seaport proved the wisdom of his choice.

His cottage stood at the water's edge, down a short lane, sandy, stony, and rutted by rains. Japanese cucumber vines and morning-glories embowered it, nearly covering the weather-stained shingles. Rows of gay hollyhocks nodded across its lower windows which commanded a full view of the harbor. This house, small and compact, about twenty-five by thirty feet square, he built in 1887. It contained a living-room, dining-room, kitchen, and three bedrooms. Its interior and decorations always reflected Tryon's refined taste and love of beauty. The mantel in the cozy living-room presented an ever-changing group of lacquers, potteries, or carvings in ivory, or tortoise-shell, which he gleaned from local sources, and many of which New Bedford whalers had brought from China or Japan. I recall at one time a considerable collection of tropical seashells which Tryon, with the help of a local fisherman, had salvaged from the sunken wreck of a schooner, bound in from southern

2

HOUSE AT SOUTH DARTMOUTH

STUDIO, SOUTH DARTMOUTH

waters. In one corner stood a fine old clock. A delicate Sheraton table supported the evening lamp, and a few well-chosen books always lay upon it. An obese black cat slept on the cushion of an old Boston rocker. An antique wheel for spinning flax served for a hatrack. Every hat on the wheel had been to sea and showed it. In the dining-room choice pieces of old blue-and-white china enlivened the sideboard, and a curious platter from Fayal, of naïve and gay design, hung above it on the wall. For many years Tryon kept in this room an early sketch of his own made at Newport, back of Bailey's Beach. One other little picture, a study of chrysanthemums, showed an unfamiliar mood in his painting.

As he prospered in his art and, as the years advanced, could easily have maintained a larger and more pretentious home, it was characteristic of him that he made no change in his mode of life in any way. He used to say, with a twinkle in his eye, 'A big house is nice, but a little house is nicer.' His shelter, clothing, and food all reflected his simple tastes. Art objects, boats, and fishing tackle were his only luxuries, and in these he did not stint himself.

A few paces from Tryon's cottage was his summer studio. It was somewhat difficult of access, for a tangle of goldenrod, blue chicory, and lusty weeds obliterated the path to it. It looked deserted. Evidently it was not a going concern. But what an admirable storehouse for spare sails, spars, fishing-tackle, and the family trunks! Here, sure enough, was an easel, looking a little out of place. A picture, too — an original Tryon. But even this solitary sign of artistic activity had a piscatorial and not merely a pictorial value. It was a life-size drawing of a striped bass. Across the dusty floor footprints led to a carpen-

3

ter shop, with a bench of tools, and racks of wood for fishing-rods seasoning overhead. Whatever the place might be, it was an enticing resort for a rainy day.

Many a pilgrim to Tryon's shrine in summer, whether art student or connoisseur, dealer or reporter, has cast curious and wistful glances at this deceptive temple. The disappointment and perplexity of those who sought admittance and were told what it contained were amusing to witness. 'Don't you ever paint or sketch in summer, Mr. Tryon?' 'Not often. At least I haven't in the last twenty or thirty years.'

But all this space for setting, and where is Tryon himself? I stated at the outset that it is fitting to come to him by the way of the sea and I have not yet found him. Is he a myth? More setting. In the harbor a hundred yachts lie at anchor, or, as the day wanes, return to their moorings, for South Dartmouth is the summer station of the New Bedford Yacht Club. The afternoon sun glows upon hulls of shining black or glittering white, on yellow and orange masts and spars, on sails of creamy Egyptian cotton. Bright ensigns and pennants quiver at mastheads and gaffs. There is a mooring near us, one of the first from the old bridge, at which swings a little round-bottomed tender. Tryon had kept it for his boats since that remote era when his was the first and only pleasure craft in Padanaram's waters.

Down the harbor toward Dumpling Light is there not a speck of white on the horizon off Mishaum Point? Unless my eyes deceive me it is the Skat. A catboat? Yes, but an aristocrat among catboats, designed by the skipper himself. She is gliding up the Nonquitt shore, wafted by the last breath of the dying sou'wester. Years of experience have made her navigator

4

so weatherwise that he calculates the life of the summer breeze to a minute, and is seldom becalmed. The little boat skillfully picks her way among the densely packed fleet. Now she takes a pilot's luff to shoot clear of a schooner yacht at anchor, now she bears away to shave by inches the stern of a crack Herreshoff sloop. Slipping through them all, she heads for her mooring buoy. Now we can hear the gentle rush and bubble of her bow wave. Even in the falling wind her lines are so fine, her sail plan so powerful, that she carries a rippling bone in her teeth.

And now, be you sailor or landsman, look sharp! Tryon picks up his mooring alone — a deft maneuver, a little test of seamanship that confirms the professional or betrays the novice. The lone figure in the Skat's cockpit suddenly puts her tiller hard down at an instant measured by split seconds. As she luffs into the wind, Tryon springs forward with the agility of a cat. Dropping on his belly, partly forward of the mast, hanging to the short bowsprit by one hand, he fends off the tender with the boathook, picks up the mooring line and makes it fast. He drops the dinghy astern, then, jumping aft to his mainsheet, he trims it smartly in and ships the boomcrotch. If you think it's easy, try it. Tryon's skies look easy, too. Let me see you paint one.

The master of the Skat puts on her sail cover and leaves her snug and shipshape for the night. He pulls up the dinghy to her quarter and lifts into it something which looks like a heavy box. With a light leap he follows, ships the oars, and rows with short quick strokes toward the opening of the draw above which we stand. The tide is ebbing against him like a millrace. When his skiff hits the swirls and eddies, he pulls madly to stem the current. He did all this at seventy as easily as he did at thirty, with or against the rushing water, for Tryon rowed under this bridge nearly every day for forty summers.

No, Tryon is not a myth. With his back to the bridge, he has as yet seen no one, but after his tussle with the tide he emerges beyond the draw, looks up and discovers my familiar face. Smiling, he exclaims, 'Why, Edward!' — the cryptic greeting traditional between us.

II

BOYHOOD

Dwight William Tryon was born in Hartford, Connecticut, August 13, 1849. He was the son of Anson Tryon and Delia O. Roberts Tryon, and he was their only child. Anson Tryon, a native of Glastonbury, Connecticut, a small country town a few miles south of Hartford on the east bank of the Connecticut River, was a builder and contractor and a skillful workman in the various details of the construction of buildings. He was especially adept in the moulding and modeling of plaster ornament, then much in vogue for ceilings and cornices, a talent which perhaps foreshadowed the sense of form so strongly developed in his son.

Genius is inexplicable and unpredictable. But it is not without possible significance that our artist was descended, on his paternal side, from several generations of craftsmen, each a skillful artisan of his kind, who lived and wrought in an age when the worker in wood or metal was an artist in his way, who took great pride in the beauty and excellence of his handiwork. From them Tryon would seem to have inherited creative impulses, and that resourcefulness and efficiency which were so

7

characteristic of New-Englanders of that time but two or three generations removed from the hardy pioneers who settled the country.

It seems that the Tryons were a family of sportsmen. Anson Tryon, with his brother Watson and other ancestors of Dwight Tryon, were all devoted to hunting and fishing. Anson Tryon was, in fact, killed while hunting with his brother by the accidental discharge of his gun as he drew it after him through a fence. At this time Dwight was about two years old.

Tryon's father probably loved the forests and streams, in his own manner, as sportsmen do. But it was his mother who bequeathed to the artist his deep imaginative love of nature. He has told me it was her habit to wander in the woods and fields by day and night, to brood upon the mystery of dawn, evening, and moonlight, responsive to the changing moods of hour and season.

Soon after the tragic event of her husband's death, Mrs. Tryon with her child returned to live at the home of her parents in East Hartford. The Roberts family were natives of this town. The father at one time had kept the country store. The family now consisted of the father and mother and an unmarried sister, Martha Roberts, of whom Tryon was very fond. 'I always have remembered my Aunt Mart,' he says,[1] 'with much affection, as a second mother who often shielded me from parental wrath and saved me from deserved punishment. In after years and until she died, upon my return to East Hartford, at long intervals and for brief periods, my aunt and I would rush into each other's arms in fond embrace, and pound

[1] This quotation, as well as the many that follow, are taken from Tryon's notes mentioned in the Preface.

BOYHOOD HOME OF TRYON

each other on the back lustily in our joy at meeting. Indeed, I think I may say that I loved her as much as my mother.'

The Roberts family were living at the time on the main street of a part of East Hartford called Hockanum, in view of the Connecticut River. The spires of the city of Hartford were visible across the river and reflected in its waters. The house was one of those old New England lean-to or salt-box types in which the rear pitch of the roof swept down nearly to the ground and formed an extension of the house at the back. It had the massive construction of its time, being framed with heavy hewn oak timbers, a foot or more square, and surrounded a great central chimney. It was over two hundred years old, and faced a sandy street through the middle of which grew a row of trees. Tryon's grandfather tilled a farm of a few acres lying back of the house.

'Of those early days,' Tryon says, 'I have few vivid or interesting memories. I attended a small village school where I acquired the three R's and little else. My pleasantest memories seem to be centered around a small stream, the outlet of the millpond, which flowed near the schoolhouse, and where, at recess, the boys rushed to explore its marvels. Here and there a deep pool, overspread by trees, afforded a tempting swimming-hole. I was cautioned by my mother not to go in swimming more than once a day, so on Saturday I went in early in the morning and stayed until night, thus living up to the letter of the law if not to the spirit. The brook babbled and sang as it ran over its pebbles, and there were all sorts of interesting life that appealed strongly to my boyish mind, and I think I got more out of it than I did from my schoolbooks.'

Tryon's ancestors on his father's side also came from this

9

section of the country, a locality called Tryontown, situated on the east side of the Connecticut River at the southern end of the Glastonbury Meadows and below what is called Naubuc. In a little hollow between the heights of the shore his grandfather built ships. The boy fished and played there.

As a schoolboy, then, up to the age of about thirteen, we find young Dwight living, on the whole, the life of the average lad in the country. But it was in his inner life that even then a profound difference was declaring itself, and he was already beginning to draw and paint. Circumstances and natural inclination tended from the first to center his attention upon the water, the millpond, the brooks and smaller streams, and the big river that flowed past the village in sight of his home. These were the favorite subjects of his early attempts. But he drew whatever came his way.

Regarding the country and landscape which surrounded Tryon in his early boyhood he says, 'It would be difficult to imagine a less interesting country, flat, sandy, and mostly given to the raising of tobacco.' Hartford offers hardly more to encourage the painter. The city and its outlying towns are situated in an alluvial plain. The Connecticut River Valley, at this point some twenty miles in width, is bounded by ranges of hills on the east and west, and the soil is fertile and easily cultivated. This region, however, is not typical of New England country, and its landscape is comparatively tame. Especially is this true of the flat plains of East Hartford, where fields of red clay or gravel, broken with stretches of dry sand, extend for miles, thickly studded with great tobacco sheds. These natural features of the landscape, combined with farmhouses rather neat and smug, and shaded by 'feather-duster' elms, offer little

10

scope for the *paysage intime*, to use the happy phrase of France. The rugged pastures of southern Connecticut, Rhode Island, and Massachusetts, on the contrary, bordering upon the sea, with their gray glacial boulders, their huckleberry, bayberry, and laurel, their sturdy oaks and old stone walls, their unkempt farms and meager soil, rich in local color, present much more inspiring material. These aroused Tryon's deepest love as a landscape painter. It was to these that he turned later for his lifelong inspiration. They touched his mind with an ever-deepening sympathy, until at last his work grew to be inseparable from such scenes.

If the landscape he knew in early childhood did not much appeal to him, he nevertheless drew and painted it occasionally. Among his earliest recollections are his drawings of the old house in which he lived, and of another farmhouse near by with an interesting background of maple trees. There was an old grist-mill, too, with an overshot wheel which he liked to draw best of all. Painters have always loved mills. The Dutchmen, and after them Turner, Constable, Bonington, were quick to feel the picturesque possibilities of these structures, now obsolete.

Tryon's fondness for the water developed early and infallibly. Less than a mile from his grandfather's door, across the meadows, the broad river flowed to the sea, and of this fact the boy was quite aware. From about 1850 to 1860 many sailing boats, sloops, schooners, scows, and barges moved daily up and down the Connecticut and afforded subjects for pencil and brush. Of these he took every advantage, and when he left East Hartford and moved with his mother to the city, he left in the old farmhouse many examples of his work as a boy. Speaking

11

of one or two that remained in his memory, he says: 'There is one in particular that I think was pretty good, considering the time at which it was done. It was in water-colors, a view of Hartford seen across our meadows, with the buildings and spires reflected in the river at evening. It hung for many years in the living-room of the old home and was much prized by the family. Another early work was a very careful drawing of the old house itself, which was also treasured by my relatives, but in the many changes that occur when homes are broken up, these early attempts of mine have been lost or destroyed. There were many in the attic of the house when I left it.'

I can testify that these early drawings and water-colors to which Tryon refers were remarkably good, considering his age and the fact that he had had few opportunities for seeing art of any kind; for he once took me to call at his old home while his relatives were still living there. The drawing of the old house hung upon the wall, together with a few other pictures done in his boyhood, and they showed an artistic sophistication, both in conception and execution, very unusual in such youthful attempts. They were unmistakably the signs and beginnings of artistic talent. It is difficult now to fix the time at which Tryon, as a child, began to draw, though it is said that he began to use a pencil at the age of four. But judging from his proficiency at the age of ten or twelve, he must have had considerable practice already. At ten, on a trip up the Hudson, he made a sketch of an island that created decided enthusiasm among the passengers. It seems safe to assume that artistic impulses were stirring in him as early as the age of five or six. In his notes he says, 'My freshest memories are of hours spent with pencil or brush in hand.'

12

We have also seen, from his own account, that his love of Nature, and especially of the water, awakened early. He had then, even as a child, made a good beginning in his career as a landscape painter. What further advantage did he need — what was his next step to be?

Hamerton, in his 'Life of Turner,' [1] says: 'When the beauty of cities and of human life in them is sufficiently perfect to satisfy the taste of a town-born artist, he will probably paint the figure, and feel but little inducement to indulge the landscape passion, if even it could become strong enough under such circumstances to produce any conscious longing. The city, then, where the landscape painter is born, ought not to be very beautiful; it ought rather to be decidedly unsatisfying to the artistic sense, and the people in it ought not to be very beautiful either. It would be well, too, if it were vast, so that the young genius should not escape from it too easily into the country, but be tormented with that aching of the heart which is the nostalgia of the lovers of Nature. Besides these conditions there is one which is absolutely essential — the child must be so situated that it will meet with the work of some previous landscape painter; for art is always in great part a tradition, even when practiced by the most original geniuses. There has never been an instance of a great artist suddenly arising in a community outside of artistic tradition. We speak loosely of artists who have lived in isolation, but the really isolated artist has never existed. This is so true that it is true even of the specialties of art. An accomplished landscape painter could never be formed where there had not been a previous gradual development of landscape painting to prepare

[1] *Life of J. M. W. Turner*, by P. G. Hamerton.

13

the way for him, and educate him, even although the community were rich in sculptors and figure painters.'

Without attaching too great importance to Hamerton's theory, it is interesting to note its application to Tryon's development as a landscape painter, for, from now on, the events of his youth curiously seem to confirm it. At the age of about thirteen, Tryon attended the high school in East Hartford and there, as he says, acquired 'a little Latin and less Greek.' Some twelve months later, he went to Hartford with his mother to live.

III

THE BOOKSTORE

Success is often attributed to luck. Some observers of Tryon's career have been inclined to emphasize the fact that Fortune always favored him. They seemed to think that, like the proverbial cat, he always landed on his feet, and that, for him, nothing happened too early or too late. His friend Bell used to say that if Tryon fell down a sewer, he would find a gold watch at the bottom. If we judge only by final results instead of seeking for first causes, I must admit that Tryon seemed to have been born under a lucky star. But surely, from the worldly point of view, Fate was not too kind to the lad of fourteen, who, with his widowed mother, arrived in the town of Hartford with their living to make, with few friends, little money, and no special trade or business by which to make more. And the boy's longing to study art must, for a time at least, remain unsatisfied. Not an encouraging outlook, certainly. But it had the advantage of sharpening the wits, of developing a native ingenuity and industry.

Colt's Firearms Factory in Hartford, then at the peak of war-time production, needed machinists. Young Tryon ap-

15

plied for a job and got it. The rudimentary training of eye and hand he had acquired in attempting to paint pictures came into play, and he served a short apprenticeship at making delicate machine tools. The time so spent was not wasted, even for the future landscape painter, for the skill gained in working with metal fitted in well with his general technical equipment of later years. Taking the first employment that offered was quite characteristic. He did not, however, remain long in the factory. Destiny had other plans for him.

At the corner of Main and Asylum Streets in the growing city was a bookstore. One evening, in the Lincoln-McClellan presidential campaign of 1864, the Republicans of Hartford had a torchlight procession. Somebody set off a rocket which exploded in a photographer's studio directly above the bookstore. The studio was ruined by fire, the bookstore and its stock damaged by water, and its proprietors held a fire sale of books. Tryon, the machinist's apprentice, scraped together a few dollars and came to buy. The Connecticut Yankee, even then, was running true to form. He was already looking for bargains — even bargains in culture. And he was also keeping an eye out for the main chance. The bookstore looked inviting to the boy; he saw a possible opportunity to improve his education and advance his fortunes. Again at a crucial point he sought employment in what seemed to him a higher field and obtained it. Brown and Gross, the booksellers, gave Tryon the position of bookkeeper and clerk which he held for ten years, from the age of fifteen to twenty-five.

You may ask how the youth of fifteen had learned to keep books. Well, for one thing, he had attended a business college evenings; and he wrote a beautiful hand. He was also

16

quick to adapt himself to changed requirements, and he soon mastered the details of his new work. As for Tryon's success in obtaining not only this situation, but others in later life, his personality undoubtedly had much to do with it. He had a genial, compelling manner. People liked him. And he always seemed to meet opportunity more than halfway. I am led to the conclusion that, after all, Tryon was lucky — in his character.

Mr. Leverett Belknap, of Hartford, two years younger than Tryon, was also a clerk in the bookstore. 'We worked together,' says Mr. Belknap, 'in the old store of Brown and Gross from 1864 until 1869, when we moved down Asylum Street to the present location. The whole stock was carried in loads on a wheelbarrow, and Tryon and I arranged it in our new quarters. All the time he was with us he showed evidences of ability and ambition. During spare moments he studied art and developed his talent. He used to keep his tubes of color in his desk and it was littered with his sketches. Years after Tryon left Hartford, his drawings of boats, in charcoal or color, decorated the walls of the basement. The whitewash brush finally obliterated them. He kept much to himself and did not join in the usual diversions of young men. But he was very fond of Nature, and on Sundays used to row down the Connecticut with another clerk and myself in a little boat he owned. Tryon would sketch the river scenery. Then we left him at Hockanum near his old home and rowed up to Hartford. Tryon walked back in the evening through East Hartford and across the old toll bridge.'

Mr. Belknap also says of Tryon: 'He attended Hannum's Business School and was adept with pen and ink. He did a good deal of scroll work which was very popular at the time. An

17

elaborately decorated temperance pledge which he did for the Pearl Street Church still exists, with the signatures of prominent citizens.' All arts and processes that tend to develop delicate perception of form as well as manual skill attracted him. But we remember that Rembrandt was a calligraphist, that Millet loved to draw letters, and that in China and Japan the man who writes beautifully is accounted an artist. Tryon became so expert in writing that he was given charge of special classes in the subject in the business school which he attended. He once said that one of his first impulses toward artistic effort came to him when he saw examples of expert penmanship and felt the desire to emulate them. In later life he asserted that there was a direct relation between the pictographic writing of the Japanese and the amazing fluency of their ink paintings.

I remember well the vivid impression made upon me when, as a boy of fourteen, I first visited Tryon's studio, by the examples of ornamental calligraphy he had about him, not only of writing, but also pen-and-ink drawings of ships and boats. There was one figure-piece in particular, a copy of an engraving by F. O. C. Darley from his Rip Van Winkle set. It represented the wanderer standing in the doorway of his house berated by his wife. The rendering in pen and ink was almost as fine as in the steel engraving itself.

This training could not fail to be helpful, in its severe discipline of form and in accuracy and delicacy of touch, as a preparation for the more systematic and scientific study of drawing which was to follow. That Tryon became very proficient in it is shown by the fact that he used to write, as a side business, not only visiting cards, but also engrossed diplomas, resolutions, legal, and, as he says, 'perhaps some illegal documents.'

18

Curiously enough there is little evidence of this early accomplishment in Tryon's later handwriting. His correspondence was always legible, though written in a small, cramped, and crabbed hand, owing, I think, to his economy of time.

Soon after young Tryon and his mother arrived in Hartford, Mrs. Tryon secured the position of custodian in the picture gallery of the Wadsworth Atheneum, an institution housed in a building erected and given to the community by a public-spirited citizen, Daniel Wadsworth. This structure was the home of an historical society, a free library, and contained a museum of antiquities, mostly early Americana and relics of the Revolutionary War; and, lastly, a gallery of paintings. While these were not of great value or interest, except historically, there were after all a few good examples of contemporary art. There were some early pictures by Frederick E. Church, who at that time had completed most of his best work. A fine portrait by Raeburn, a portrait of Benjamin West, by Sir Thomas Lawrence, and a view of Mount Etna by Thomas Cole, gave character to the otherwise mediocre collection.

The picture gallery was a sepulchral chamber. The dim light filtered down from an opening in the lofty ceiling as into a well. The place had a musty odor. One spoke in whispers, for one's voice echoed with a grim and startling effect. When, in boyhood, I wandered into the gallery, after exchanging my books at the adjoining library, it was usually deserted, except for the solitary figure of Tryon's mother, who, as attendant, sat at a small table, sold tickets, and distributed catalogues. The old pictures excited my wonder and admiration, as they did Tryon's when he first saw them. But a little comedy that was occasionally enacted in these dignified and somewhat forbidding surroundings greatly enlivened them for me. At the end of the room, near the entrance, stood Bartholomew's life-size statue of 'Eve Repentant.' I was enchanted by it, but there was one discordant note. On the pedestal, at Eve's feet, lay the fateful apple, showing plainly the bite she had taken; and near it, the tail of the serpent entwined the rock upon which she sat. Strangely enough, both the apple and the tail were colored a rich golden amber, in sharp contrast to the white purity of Eve's lovely figure. Not quite as highly polished as the worn toe of Saint Peter, in his church in Rome, but noticeable, nevertheless. I was puzzled to account for it. And then, one day, as I stood looking at the pictures, a band of five or six dirty little street gamins stole quietly up the stairs, tiptoed to the statue, and each in turn quickly rubbed his grimy paws over the marble apple and the scales of the snake.

Mrs. Tryon, sitting with her back to the statue, did not see or hear them; but as the last urchin took his final rub, she evidently scented danger. She turned, rose, and as she advanced upon them, the little hoodlums raced for the stairs and tore madly out with shrill whoops of derision. I witnessed several such scenes. But I did not then know that I had solved the problem of the patina on the statues of the Loggia dei Lanzi, which is measured by the height to which the human hand can reach.

Tryon, of course, often visited the gallery to see his mother, and had what was then the advantage of intimate contact with the pictures. We can imagine the boy's interest in the old paintings, the first of any importance he had ever seen. I must not forget another early source of inspiration. James G. Batterson, an enterprising and successful citizen of Hartford, the

CATALOGUE

OF

PAINTINGS

IN

Wadsworth Gallery,

HARTFORD.

ADMITTANCE FOR ONE PERSON, 15 CENTS.

CHILDREN UNDER 14 YEARS OF AGE, 10 CENTS.

ANNUAL TICKET FOR ONE PERSON, $1.

ANNUAL TICKET TO ADMIT THE MEMBERS OF ONE FAMILY, $2.50.

ANNUAL TICKET FOR A FAMILY, WITH THE PRIVILEGE OF INTRODU-
CING THEIR FRIENDS FROM OUT OF TOWN, $3.50.

THE PICTURES

ARE NOT TO BE TOUCHED WITH PARASOLS, CANES OR THE FINGERS.

Umbrellas, Parasols, Canes and Whips to be left at the head of the Stairs.

Hartford:

PRESS OF CASE, TIFFANY AND COMPANY.

1856.

CATALOGUE, WADSWORTH ATHENÆUM, 1856

organizer and first president of the Travelers Insurance Company, had purchased in Europe a small collection of Dutch paintings which were exhibited at the Atheneum Gallery. They consisted of Dutch coast scenes and views of shipping, cattle on sunny meadows, and skaters on frozen canals. There were still-life and genre pictures among them and landscapes with sheep by Koek-Koek. Although a trifle old-fashioned to our modern taste, they seemed wonderful to young Tryon. They immediately fired his imagination and filled him with a desire to emulate them.

Here, then, we find Tryon, a year or two after his arrival in Hartford from the country, established in business as book-keeper and clerk for Brown and Gross, as I have said. The year was 1864. He regarded this event as the true beginning of his serious education. With some leisure, especially through the summer months when customers were less numerous, and with the wealth of literature at hand, he began a course of general reading which became a fixed habit of his life. The many finely illustrated books on art he found there opened to him, as he says, 'a new world of beauty,' and he considered the experience more valuable than a college education would have been. As we shall see in future chapters, his reading was to have a marked effect, not only upon the development of his mind, but on his knowledge of art in general, and his taste and discrimination as an artist.

Tryon's early efforts had been chiefly confined to black and white and to water-color. He continued to work in the latter medium more and more as opportunity offered, and from this to painting in oil was but a step. As his daily occupation in the bookstore left him little time to devote to sketching from nature, he early formed the habit of painting from memory such out-of-door subjects as interested him. In this way he acquired one of the most valuable faculties that a landscape painter can possess.

The youth read widely in his leisure moments the classic works of history, fiction, poetry, and the fine arts, in the stock of the store; and on Sundays and holidays worked industriously at his painting, in which he was rapidly acquiring considerable facility. In fact, his work already began to attract attention and occasionally he sold a picture. His first patron was William Bailey Faxon, the artist, who was about Tryon's age and of similar tastes, and who was to study art in Paris with him a few years later.

Tryon had painted a little Venetian marine in oil about six by eight inches, finely composed, inspired by a reproduction of a Turner. With his usual business instinct he had put it in the window of a frame-maker, near the bookstore, and set the price at fifteen dollars. It happened that Mr. Faxon had just received gifts of a gold watch and a ten-dollar gold piece, on his twenty-first birthday. Strolling along Asylum Street, Tryon's picture took his eye. 'I entered the bookstore,' says Mr. Faxon, 'and told Tryon how much I admired it. But,' I said, 'your price is fifteen dollars and I have only ten. If the picture is not sold, would you let me have it for that, as I can think of nothing I would like better for my birthday?' Tryon, always pleased by appreciation of his work, readily agreed, and his first sale was effected. This was in the year 1870.

And now comes a slight digression, the only wavering that Tryon ever showed in his otherwise straight line of progress. At the outset of his career he hesitated for a brief moment between art and medicine as a profession. With all his poetic and imaginative qualities he had a strongly scientific turn of mind which was to be an important factor in his technical skill. The human organism, with its wondrous beauty, its marvelous mechanism, intensely interested him. He started to study medicine and surgery and read extensively upon these subjects. He did not pursue them long, but long enough to master anatomy, which especially fascinated him, so that later, when he arrived at the École des Beaux Arts in Paris, the anatomical course was but child's play for him.

We gather from Mr. Belknap, Tryon's associate in business, that the young man was reserved, industrious, and not much given to conventional diversions.- But he was not entirely unsocial, and he began to make friends with interesting young people in Hartford, some of whom, like himself, were later to make their mark in the world. Otis Skinner, the actor, was one of these.

In his book of reminiscences of the stage,[1] Mr. Skinner writes: 'One holiday I look back upon with unalloyed delight. It was a walking tour through the Berkshires with Dwight W. Tryon. His fame as a landscape painter had not then spread beyond Hartford. A primrose by a river's brim had always been a yellow primrose to me, but in his enthusiasm I saw with new eyes. Often we would halt by hill or stream and, while he sketched the spot that intrigued him, I propped my elbows on the grass and studied my play-book.'

Such knowledge as Tryon had, at this time, of drawing and painting he had gleaned from books on the subject which he had at his command, and from his own practice. When he

[1] *Footlights and Spotlights*, by Otis Skinner. Bobbs-Merrill Company, 1924.

seriously began to paint, he had seen very few good pictures. Most of the work which found its way to Hartford was of the so-called Hudson River School. Occasionally a W. T. Richards or an early Wyant appeared in the local art store and interested him as being a step in advance of the average painting then to be seen. He studied them closely and their influence is felt in his early works of this period. .

As I have noted, our young artist now began to sell the pictures he painted in his spare time. The short summer vacations of a week or two which were allowed him gave him further opportunity which he used diligently. In fact, he exhibited at the National Academy of Design — in New York at this time. 'I remember well,' he says, 'the pleasure I felt on being notified that my water-color, "Gunning Rock — Narragansett Pier," had been purchased by Samuel P. Avery, a well-known collector.' The following winter Tryon again exhibited, at the same institution, a large oil entitled 'The Coast of Maine — East Wind.' This was also sold in New York City.

In this year, 1873, Tryon married Miss Alice H. Belden, of Hartford, the daughter of Seabury and Celestia Belden. She shared the early years of struggle and hardship with him, and in Paris their little home in the Latin quarter was a rendezvous and refuge for his unmarried student friends. It had no trace of the Bohemian chaos that sometimes accompanies the artistic temperament, but then, as always, was charming in its well-ordered comfort and repose. They had no children. Mrs. Tryon died on October 27, 1929.

As Tryon approached the end of the decade spent in the bookstore, ever more interested in painting and encouraged by the success he had already achieved, he felt that he was ap-

SCENE IN THE WHITE MOUNTAINS

proaching a parting of the ways. He knew the time had come to choose between business and art. He had saved enough money to tide him along for a time, so, in 1873, at the age of twenty-four, he decided definitely that art was to be his profession. He abandoned business life forever and took a studio in Hartford.

IV

THE HARTFORD STUDIO

THE conditions of life in the city of Hartford, at the time Tryon opened his studio, have their significance as a part of his youthful environment. Hartford was then a provincial New England town of about thirty thousand inhabitants. Its business activities still centered around the intersection of Main and Asylum Streets, with the fine old Bulfinch State House of the Revolutionary period dominating the scene. Many dignified and charming old residences remained interspersed among the commercial structures. Stages, soon to be followed by horse-drawn street cars, plied north and south through the main thoroughfare at leisurely intervals. Even in the busy section the stately elms under which the youth used to walk still graced the streets.

For several years Tryon had enjoyed some rather unusual friendships and intellectual opportunities. About five or six years before he gave up the bookshop, an interesting group of literary folk and of distinguished preachers and lawyers made their homes in Hartford. Some of the clergymen of the city were men of more than local reputation. There was Horace

26

Bushnell, a prominent figure in the Congregational Church, a preacher of great distinction and of broad and liberal views relatively to his time; and the Reverend Doctors Joseph H. Twichell, Edwin P. Parker, and Nathaniel J. Burton completed a somewhat noted ecclesiastical quartet.

In the year 1871, Mark Twain, then thirty-six years old, had moved to Hartford and built a fine residence on Farmington Avenue. Professor Stowe and Harriet Beecher Stowe, his wife, the author of 'Uncle Tom's Cabin,' lived near by on Forest Street. Charles Dudley Warner was Mark Twain's nearest neighbor. The bookstore in which Tryon was employed was unusually good. The literary people frequented it daily, and there Tryon met and knew Mark Twain, Warner, Mrs. Stowe, and Doctors Bushnell, Burton, Twichell, and Parker. Through these Tryon became acquainted with other writers and people of note. Mark Twain, however, seems to have taken an especial interest in him. He sought him out in the store and sometimes invited him to his house to play billiards. And probably he took some interest in his diversion of painting. But when the youth announced that he was going to give up business and devote himself to art, Mark Twain drew the line. He went straight to the bookstore. 'Tryon,' said he, falling into the inimitable drawl, 'Tryon, you are making the mistake of your life! Here you are earning an honest and comfortable living, and, like a fool, you throw it up for a career in art, which of all things in the world is the most fickle. You will probably starve to death in a garret.'

The Reverend Joseph Twichell, too, strongly advised Tryon to stick to business and predicted disaster if he persisted in his determination to become a painter. For a time it looked as if

27

the young man was to meet his fate without benefit of clergy. Though with one exception. Dr. Horace Bushnell had a wider vision and he came to the rescue with other counsel. He encouraged Tryon in his ambition, adding sage observations upon artistic matters and upon life in general. Tryon relates that Dr. Bushnell said to him, later on: 'Tryon, I'm glad you are going abroad to study. The fault with most artists is that they have untrained minds. The cow in the field has as good optics as we, but sees nothing but grass.'

It is pleasing to record that many years afterward, when Tryon had achieved success, Mark Twain made full admission that he had been mistaken in his prophecies. Dr. Twichell, too, in his later life, went on one occasion to Smith College to visit one of his daughters who was studying there with Tryon, then internationally known as a painter. The clergyman sought out the artist, congratulated him on his success, and recalled with amusement how he had once warned him against adopting art as a profession.

Tryon's decision to give up business and launch his barque upon the adventurous sea of art seems natural enough to us now, as we view it in the light of subsequent events. We must, however, recall something of the general attitude of mind of New England people of that day toward art and artists to realize what a momentous thing it was for a young man to do. Artists, like actors, were looked at a little askance, and, with the possible exception of the portrait painter, were not considered indispensable to the welfare of any well-regulated community. Painting pictures was hardly one of the useful occupations, certainly not a gainful one. And if a literary personage like Mark Twain disapproved of young Tryon's adventure,

28

CLAY CLIFFS, BLOCK ISLAND, SUNSET

what must more staid and practical people have thought of it? Probably as visionary, and also a little *déclassé* in its assumed Bohemian aspects. But most certainly as frivolous. 'Let joy be unconfined' was not the motto of our New England ancestors.

> 'Passion is here a soilure of the wits,
> We're told, and Love a cross for them to bear;
> Joy shivers in the corner where she knits,
> And Conscience always has the rocking chair,
> Cheerful as when she tortured into fits
> The first cat that was ever killed by Care.'

So sings a New England poet of these later years.[1] But Tryon had the courage of his convictions; he was enterprising and adventurous. And, although he saw visions and dreamed dreams, his inheritance of good sense and practicality never deserted him. He had no sooner opened his studio in Hartford than he made it known that he would give instruction in drawing and painting. He had made the acquaintance of the Cheney family, the wealthy silk manufacturers of South Manchester, Connecticut. They became his friends and patrons and so remained for many years. They gave him substantial aid when he went abroad to study. Colonel Frank Cheney had married Mary Bushnell, daughter of Dr. Horace Bushnell, who, with her sister, afterward Mrs. Hillyer, inherited many of her father's intellectual traits and gifts. Both these cultured women had a deep interest in art. The younger members of the Cheney family came at once to Tryon for instruction in drawing and painting. Others joined his classes and he was assured of a modest livelihood, without counting on the sale of his pictures. He always had an anchor to windward.

[1] From Edwin Arlington Robinson's sonnet, 'New England.'

About this time Tryon went to Mount Desert, where he stayed three months and made many studies. From them he later painted several ambitious pictures, among them 'Eagle Lake, Morning Mist,' 'Green Mountain from Otter Creek,' and 'Surf, South-East Point.' Much to his surprise all of these pictures found purchasers, so that, as he says, 'the day of starvation was postponed for a time.' Later in the same year he went to the White Mountains and saw them clothed in all the glory of autumn colors. From the studies he made there he also painted several pictures. Perhaps the best of these were 'The White Hills from Jefferson,' 'Evening Light,' and 'The Meadows of Conway.' [1]

The following summer he spent at Block Island, then little known or frequented by artists. He made many studies of the cliffs and the south shore and from one of them he later painted an important picture called 'Clay Cliffs, Block Island — Sunset.' It was painted for exhibition at the Centennial Exposition of 1876. It stood upon an easel in Tryon's studio when I first met him, and he had just completed it. It presented the first and most striking object that met my eye as I entered the door, and impressed me deeply. It showed the steep and rugged red clay cliffs of the south shore of Block Island rising at the right in the composition, with the last rays of the sun, setting in a bluish mist at the left, glowing upon them with great richness and depth of color. The surf, painted with vigor and feeling, beat and broke upon the beach in the foreground. This picture, a large canvas, is still owned in Hartford. Seeing it not long ago and after an interval of fifty years, its power and beauty struck me vividly again. Considering the comparatively short time

[1] I do not know where these pictures now are or by whom owned.

that Tryon had been painting when he produced this work, it is singularly full and mature, a remarkable achievement for so young an artist.

Tryon resided in Hartford until 1876, working hard at his painting. Our friendship of nearly a lifetime dates from this period. So perhaps this is as good a place as any to set down in some detail what was to me a very significant experience. The year was 1875. Tryon was now twenty-six years old and stood at the threshold of a great career in his chosen profession.

Upon what was then the top floor of the Connecticut Mutual Insurance Building in Hartford, at the corner of Main and Pearl Streets, several artists had studios. Among them was the portrait painter William R. Wheeler, a man of more than average talent. In the tower of the southeast corner of the building, since rebuilt, was the studio of Tryon. A couple of lads whose father was employed in the building were schoolboy friends of mine, and on Saturdays I used to go there with them. We played about the buildings and enjoyed the fine view of the city, the river, and East Hartford to be seen from a large window on the top floor. I loved nature and had already begun to draw and paint. One memorable day the door of Tryon's studio stood ajar, and I caught a glimpse of pictures which drew me like a magnet. I ventured nearer, and a voice said, 'Come in.' I needed no second invitation and we were soon engaged in an interesting conversation during which I managed to tell him of my great desire to learn to draw and paint. He assured me that, if my parents were willing, he would be glad to help me. For the remainder of that winter I worked in his studio every Saturday, and when summer came he invited me to accompany him to Block Island on a sketching trip. My

31

parents, however, becoming alarmed at the idea that I was making progress under his instruction and foreseeing the possible danger that I might take to art as a profession, refused permission. I have long since forgiven them, but I shall carry the memory of my disappointment to my grave.

Tryon's habits of work and play, consistent throughout his career, were already firmly fixed at the time of our first meeting. His love of nature, and particularly of the water, was strongly developed. From the time of his childhood, when he improvised his first really seaworthy boat out of an old wooden sink, discarded from the house, he had always gone upon the water. At the time I now record he had a rowing shell on the Connecticut River. Fencing was another of his hobbies and he often appeared at the studio with a pair of foils. He played billiards a good deal. This game he always liked, for it afforded a field for his peculiar gifts of quick judgment of eye and delicate manual skill.

He told me that he got his first acquaintance with salt water when he was about eighteen years old. He made two trips in a little schooner that plied between Hartford and Provincetown, taking apples and bringing back codfish. And in a smack he made a voyage in Long Island Sound, fished for bluefish in Plum Gut and touched at Block Island. 'I enjoyed it all immensely,' said he. 'It made a deep impression upon me. And I have always remembered when, in an easterly gale we had to put in back of Monomoy, how the mate felt his way in by taking the soundings of the bottom from the lead, as he was unfamiliar with the coast.'

Tryon had found his true element. Afterward he often shipped as foremast hand on fishing smacks or coasting schoon-

32

EARLY DRAWING, ABOUT 1870

ers and apprenticed himself for short trips to the market fishermen of the New England coast, to hoist in the inglorious cod or handline flounders and tautog. And the rough life in those days, the cramped bunks in the fo'c'sle, the hard fare, the labor and exposure, held the index to his future habits and laid the foundation of his iron constitution. Tryon was of Spartan mould. He used to say, speaking of hardships: 'I have been in some tough places in my life, where the living was primitive and the fare meager, almost to the point of starvation, but I have always found I could live where any one else could. I ate codfish and potatoes and nothing else all one summer in a fisherman's hut at Mount Desert, and came out as thin as a rail in the fall, but I survived.'

His interest in the sea and life upon it now showed itself in many minute and beautiful drawings of ships and boats, done in pencil, crayon, and pen and ink, as well as in his more important marines. Much to my delight he often gave me one of these to copy.

Tryon continued to paint and exhibit both in Hartford and in New York during the years 1874, 1875, and part of 1876. He sold his pictures readily, though for small prices, and his classes in drawing and painting increased in numbers, assuring him a modest income sufficient for his wants. This peaceful life could not long continue. He became aware of a divine discontent.

V

THE PARIS YEARS

Commenting upon the events of those years and of his desire for further study, Tryon says:

'While greatly encouraged by the reception my work had received, I realized that there was something lacking in all art work being produced in this country. From Europe and especially from France came pictures which had a breadth and power which were most convincing. At this time, about 1875, the art schools of the United States offered inadequate instruction, and I decided to go abroad and take advantage of the schools there, and, if necessary, of the criticisms and help of individual painters and teachers.

'To this end I gathered all my pictures and sketches and held an exhibition and sale at auction of the unsold work. This was the autumn of 1876.

'When all was settled, I found myself in the possession of what seemed the inexhaustible sum of about two thousand dollars.

'With this great amount of money, and with the boundless hope of youth, my wife and I sailed on the fourth of December,

34

1876, for France *via* Liverpool. We left New York in a mantle of snow, and I remember being impressed by seeing, all the way from Liverpool to London, green fields with farmers at work, some ploughing and others engaged in various agricultural tasks.

'On our arrival at Paris we were escorted by an artist friend to a small hotel opposite the École des Beaux Arts, where we remained temporarily until we found a cozy apartment of three rooms in the Rue Guy Lussac.

'Here in the heart of the Latin Quarter, I at once took up the life of the art student. Every morning before eight, I took my way down the Rue de Seine to a crèmerie, where I had my "quatre sous de chocolat" and a bun, and then to the studio of Jacquesson de la Chevreuse in the Rue Bonaparte. In his studio I found a number of Americans whom I knew, some French students, and some from central European states.

'Jacquesson de la Chevreuse, a favorite pupil of Ingres, handed down and taught the severe principles of that great master. While such severely classical and academic methods of instruction might seem, at first thought, unrelated to my work as a confirmed landscape painter, I found the discipline most valuable.

'I worked three winters in this studio, mornings from life and afternoons from casts, and at the École des Beaux Arts I attended lectures on architecture, anatomy, and history. I also studied a short time with Harpignies and Charles Daubigny, but received little help from them, though I formed a pleasant association and friendship.'

It is true, as Tryon has stated in his notes, that the facilities for the study of art in this country had been, up to this time, inadequate. The first American students to seek wider opportunities in Europe had gone to Rome, Munich, or Düsseldorf. Then Paris became the recognized art center, and among the older men, John La Farge, George Inness, and William Morris Hunt went there to study, to be followed later by Kenyon Cox, Abbott H. Thayer, Tryon, Dewing, Brush, Low, the two Weirs, and a number of others. Some of them returning home in 1877 founded the Society of American Artists with John La Farge as president. Contemporaneously, another group of American students, including William M. Chase, Frank Duveneck, Walter Shirlaw, and Joseph Decamp, were studying in Munich under Piloty and other German masters. They, too, returning to America, became charter members of the Society of American Artists.

Tryon arrived in Paris in 1876 at a time when the academic and classical traditions of French painting had waned. Though some of the painters of the Barbizon School, or men of 1830, were still living and working, most of them were either dead or near the end of their lives and accomplishment. Corot and Millet had been dead but a year, Rousseau about eight years. Of the others Daubigny, Diaz, and Dupré were still living. In this very year Whistler, at this time forty-two years old, was living in London. The works of Manet, Monet, Renoir, Pissaro, Sisley, and others of the early Impressionists, began to influence the younger painters and turned their attention to technical problems of broken and vibrated color, high key, luminosity, and the methods of so-called *plein-air* painting. These at that time seemed revolutionary, though as a matter of fact Turner had achieved many beautiful and brilliant effects of light and color years before by similar means.

36

But while not unmindful of the momentous events in the art life of Paris during his student days, Tryon seems to have been but slightly influenced by the fads or sensationalism of the moment. He at once settled down to work, and devoted his energies, with the directness that was characteristic of him, to the acquirement of a sound education in painting. We must also remember that, as Caffin says of him, 'When Tryon reached Paris, his mind was formed beyond the average of students.... He had a fixed purpose, and a clear understanding also of what he needed to attain it. He had the warrantable belief in himself that belongs to a self-made man. He had proved that he could do things, and he had developed a clear conviction of what he meant to do.' Then, too, the fact that he was married and settled in domestic life when he arrived in Europe was exceptional for an art student. That also tended to stabilize him and enabled him to pursue his studies free from the distractions common to student life in the Latin Quarter. Tryon has told me that while studying in Paris there were many forces to pull him about in different directions; that the new movements in painting were distracting; but that he held firmly to the one thing he had in mind, and kept a clear head and single purpose through it all.

At that time most of the American students sought the big and crowded ateliers of Boulanger and Lefebvre, Gérôme, Jean Paul Laurens, Julien and Carolus Duran, but Tryon, with an instinct which ever served him, learned, soon after his arrival, of the small but highly specialized drawing school of Jacquesson de la Chevreuse. While the larger and more popular schools were either free or charged but a nominal tuition fee, 'Jackson's,' as it was familiarly known to the students, admitted but few pupils, and was comparatively expensive. Tryon soon saw that in the larger studios the criticisms were infrequent, little time was given to the individual student, and they were mostly dependent for help upon their more advanced companions. Contrariwise, at Jacquesson's the number of pupils was restricted, the criticisms constant, scientifically thorough, and adapted to the needs of the individual. Progress was rapid. Though Tryon's means were limited, he decided, with native shrewdness, that the best was the cheapest, and entered the more select school. Jacquesson de la Chevreuse was by nature and training a remarkable teacher of the science of drawing. A favorite pupil of Ingres, he had achieved honor in the realm of painting. At one time the Prix de Rome had been his had not ill-health prevented his taking it. Teaching, however, seems to have had a great attraction for him, and indeed he had a genius for it. To Tryon's keen and analytic mind the severely scientific methods of Jacquesson's academy appealed strongly. When he submitted examples of his work to the master, Jacquesson said, 'You draw very well, but your work lacks system.'

Accordingly for three winters our young searcher for truth humbly threw aside what was a considerable accomplishment for so young a man, together with established habits of work of his preceding years at home, and entirely reconstructed his approach to drawing. He was a conscientious and tireless worker and in six months was advanced from the antique to the life class. He rapidly assimilated those principles and methods which were to establish his art upon an enduring basis. The Connecticut Yankee had married his restless energy and native ingenuity to French science and discipline, a union which was to be prolific in interesting offspring.

38

THE CNIDIAN VENUS, CAST DRAWING

The beautiful cast and life drawings, in the collection of Tryon's work at Smith College, are revelations of the mastery of form — of line, of mass, of values — with atmospheric envelopment never neglected. They show supremely into what subtleties the study of pure form can be carried. Such severely classical and academic ideals might seem, as Tryon has said, unrelated to his work as a landscape painter. But the anatomy and structure which, like granite ledges, underlie the poetry and mystery of his landscapes, are the direct result of this searching study of form. That he should have understood intuitively the vital importance of this training, to an artist who was to go far in his profession, seems a part of what many people who knew him have termed his luck. Really it is, however, only an example of his perception and appropriation of anything essential to his inner development.

It is interesting to note here that Whistler, whose painting in some of its phases had a kinship with Tryon's, regretted that he was denied the severe discipline of the Ingres tradition. I quote the following letter of Whistler's to his friend Fantin Latour because it reveals not only the importance that Whistler attached to the kind of training which Tryon received, but also for the reason that it is such an excellent exposition of the relation of form to color. As a contribution to our knowledge M. Bénédite quoted in the 'Gazette des Beaux Arts' a letter written to Fantin in the sixties:

'I have far too many things to tell you for me to write them all this morning, for I am in an impossible press of work. It is the pain of giving birth. You know what that is. I have several pictures in my head and they issue with difficulty. For I must tell you that I am grown exacting and "difficile" — very differ-

39

ent from what I was when I threw everything pell-mell on canvas, knowing that instinct and fine color would carry me through. Ah! my dear Fantin, what an education I have given myself! or, rather, what a fearful want of education I am conscious of! With the fine gifts I naturally possess, what a painter I should now be, if, vain and satisfied with those powers, I hadn't disregarded everything else. You see, I came at an unfortunate moment. Courbet and his influence were odious. The regret, the rage, even the hatred I feel for all that now would perhaps astonish you, but here is the explanation. It isn't poor Courbet that I loathe, nor even his works. I recognize, as I always did, their qualities. Nor do I lament the influence of his painting on mine. There isn't any; none will be found in my canvases. That can't be otherwise, for I am too individual and have always been rich in qualities which he hadn't and which were enough for me. But this is why all that was so bad for me. That damned realism made such a direct appeal to my vanity as a painter, and, flouting all traditions, shouted with the assurance of ignorance, "Vive la Nature!" "Nature," my boy — that cry was a piece of bad luck for me. My friend, our little society was as refractory as you like. Oh! why wasn't I a pupil of Ingres? I don't say that in rapture before his pictures. I don't care much for them. I think a lot of his paintings that we saw together very questionable in style, not in the least Greek, as people pretend, but very viciously French. I feel there is much more to discover, there are much finer things to do. But, I repeat it, why wasn't I his pupil? What a master he would have been. How safely he would have led us. Drawing, by Jove! Color — color is vice. Certainly it can be and has the right to be one of the finest virtues. Grasped with a strong

40

hand, controlled by her master, Drawing, color is a splendid bride with a husband worthy of her — her lover but her master, too — the most magnificent mistress in the world, and the result is to be seen in all the lovely things produced from this union. But coupled with indecision, with a weak, timid, vicious drawing, easily satisfied, color becomes a jade making game of her mate, you know, and abusing him just as she pleases, taking the thing lightly so long as she has a good time, treating her unfortunate companion like a duffer who bores her — which is just what he does. And look at the result; a chaos of intoxication, of trickery, regret, unfinished things. Well, enough of this. It explains the immense amount of work I am now doing. I have been teaching myself thus for a year and more, and I am sure that I shall make up the wasted time. But — but — what labor and pain!'

Fancy Whistler sighing for Ingres as a master! Despite the dictum in his letter, it was under the influence of Courbet, which he at once both denied and abhorred, that the 'Blue Wave' and one or two other master works were painted.

Tryon said that in Jacquesson's school all learned to draw well, for the scientific principles so seldom defined elsewhere put the pupils through a rapid forcing process that ended inevitably in good draftsmanship. An elderly Parisian with a fondness for art came into the class merely to spend his leisure time agreeably, as an amateur. He learned to draw well almost in spite of himself. Jacquesson de la Chevreuse's method of instruction, so direct, so simple, enabled the student to master quickly the principles of the representation of nature, as a means to an end and not an end in itself.

Briefly stated, the principles of drawing of the antique which

41

he taught were the grasping of the large proportions of the cast, in the simplest aspect, observing carefully the action; and insistence that the drawing should be the exact size of the cast, with careful measurements of the model itself for verification. Next, the laying in of the large masses of shadow in one simple tone, as soon as the general proportions were approximated, since the spotting of the masses at once helps the eye to perceive the true proportions and to make corrections. Then, by a rapid but careful revision of proportions and masses together, and the indication of the principal values, the whole drawing was worked upon and the relations of parts maintained. At the last such elaboration and study of details were added as would not disturb the unity of the whole.

Although he gave due importance to clearness and beauty of line, Jacquesson emphasized the losing of edges, the merging of contours and forms one into another, and laid stress upon modeling by masses and values. The final result was an atmospheric envelopment of form and analysis of light and shadow carried much farther than in most schools.

That these principles were also taught in other studios in Paris in those days goes without saying, but in this unique academy of Jacquesson's their application was particularly thorough and systematic. I may be allowed to give personal testimony at this point. Having myself studied in New York in the eighties under men who were pupils of the larger Parisian schools, and having been for some years also a student with Tryon, I could not fail to note the difference between them in theory, in practice, and especially in thoroughness. Two days a week of study with Tryon were worth a month at either of the two leading schools in New York, where the foremost of the younger men, just back from Europe, were teaching, and where the instruction was relatively excellent.

Tryon used to say that, given ordinary intelligence, he could teach any one to draw in a few months. Drawing he claimed was a mental, not a manual, process. It was a thinking of the object upon the paper. Color was another affair entirely, emotional, and could not be imparted, though it, too, had its science.

Along with Tryon in Jacquesson's school were the Americans, Robert Brandegee, Montague Flagg, and his brother Charles, and William Bailey Faxon. These men formed a select group and were more serious workers than many of those in the larger schools. Mr. Faxon, who went to Paris a year before Tryon did and who studied with him in Jacquesson's school, says that there were not more than ten or twelve students in the class. He says: 'We were all hard workers. We began at eight in the morning and painted until dark. At first we also attended the Petit École in the evening and drew and painted there. This, however, soon proved to be too strenuous, even for us, and we had to give it up. Tryon, especially, was very hard-working and studious. He did not mingle at all in the gay life of the quarter. He saved his money for travel and the sketching trips which he took each summer. We were at Cancale together one summer and at La Houle, a few miles from St. Malo.'

Hard workers they may have been, but they also indulged occasionally in a little skylarking as is the wont of art students everywhere. Tryon relates that one of their number, a newcomer, had a theory of his own about starting his drawing. He began it with an elaborate system of dots or points which took a good deal of time to place before he finally connected them by lines. Brandegee, who was something of a joker, took advan-

43

tage of this person's temporary absence from the room to change the position of *one* of the dots on his drawing, which entirely upset the scheme and obliged the unfortunate theorist to begin all over again.

Tryon was attracted at this stage of his student life to the work of Daubigny. He took some of his work and presented himself one day at Daubigny's studio in Paris, at that time in the Rue Notre Dame de Lorette. It is easy to see why Daubigny's free and vigorous handling of pigment and its direct and fresh rendering of the objective phases of nature appealed to him. Tryon felt that the criticism of such a man might be helpful to a student. It seemed to him, however, that Daubigny's painting had little subtlety and was not the product of a deep thinker. Tryon writes in an article on Daubigny, in Vandyke's book, 'Modern French Painters': 'Daubigny possessed little of the critical faculty and as often asked me for an opinion of his own work as he offered me one upon mine, and though I enjoyed his friendship and simple, kindly nature as a man, I got little help from him in my painting.'

Nevertheless, Tryon's work of this period shows slightly the influence of Daubigny, both in some of the pictures he sent home from Paris, and in those painted soon after his return, particularly in a series of moonlights. This reminiscence of the French painter lasted but a short time and never reappeared. Tryon's preoccupations with his own problems soon engrossed him, and he struck the note that was to run, with increasing strength and wider variations, through all his succeeding achievement. He refers also in his notes to the criticisms of his student work by Harpignies, which he found no more inspiring or helpful than those of Daubigny.

44

TRYON AND THAYER AT GUERNSEY, 1877

At the left are Mr. and Mrs. Tryon. In the center beside them Mr. and Mrs. Thayer

Tryon's account of his acquaintance with Daubigny is interesting, however, as it throws light upon Daubigny's method of painting and upon his character as a man. Tryon describes him as an honest and simple soul living the life of a farmer or sailor, wholly absorbed in his art and his love of the country. He worked almost entirely from nature, at least for the first painting. He often took his sketch home and, by a little touching up, developed it into a finished picture in the studio. Many or most of his smaller pictures were painted in this way. The rivers Seine, Marne, and Oise were among Daubigny's sketching grounds, and he lived much of his time upon a sort of combined houseboat and studio which he moved about from one quiet nook or interesting stretch of a river to another, as the subject or his mood invited. His favorite haunt was the Oise.

The French landscape painter J. B. A. Guillemet, however, who was a pupil of Corot and Oudinot, gave Tryon some substantial aid. His criticisms were constructive and pertinent, and Tryon's acquaintance with him was an interesting episode. This artist, whose work ranks with the best of modern landscape painting, seems never to have had the reputation he deserves in comparison with many of his contemporaries, at least in this country. He has been little known among our connoisseurs, or dealers, and the best of his work remains abroad. He painted large impressive canvases. His 'Cliffs at Dieppe' and 'Paris from Bercy,' the latter for a time in the Luxembourg, are dignified and beautiful pictures, imposing and dramatic. Guillemet's landscapes greatly attracted Tryon by their truth and vigor, and he found the artist not only a charming personality but a stimulating influence. Although Guillemet was not a teacher, his comments upon Tryon's work were terse and very much to the point. He seized at once and unerringly upon the faults in a picture. With equal insight he dwelt upon its merits. He called one day at Tryon's studio and found him out. A picture called 'Harvest Time in Normandy' which Tryon had painted for the Salon stood upon an easel. Guillemet wrote upon a panel '*Bon tableau!* Fine in tone, *très jolie!* The foreground a little harsh and crude.'

In Tryon's account of his acquaintance with this artist he mentions the fact that, although Guillemet mostly painted large pictures, often five or six by eight or ten feet in size, curiously enough his studio measured about twelve by fourteen feet. In order to see his picture as a whole he had a large mirror at the end of the room facing his easel by which he thus obtained the effect of greater distance.

Guillemet was a well-known figure in the art world of Paris in those days. His portrait appears in a picture by Manet called 'Le Balcon,' shown in the Salon of 1869. His influence upon the young American is not negligible, and Tryon always referred to the acquaintance with pleasure and satisfaction and said, 'Guillemet gave me much wise advice and was well fitted to direct me out of certain academic paths into which I had fallen from study in the schools.'

VI

FOREIGN INFLUENCES

Of the further happenings of his sojourn abroad Tryon says: 'As Jacquesson's studio was closed for the summers, it left us free to plan sketching trips to the country. The first summer, 1877, we spent in the island of Guernsey. With Abbott H. Thayer, his wife and baby Mary, and an artist from London, Arthur H. Bell, we hired a cottage in that garden-like spot.'

This was the beginning of the lifelong friendship between Tryon and Thayer. Thayer at this time was painting animals. A photograph exists of the little cottage doorway where the two artists are seated in a group with their wives, their friend, and their Guernsey hosts. Tryon told me that while they were walking along the coast in Guernsey one day, he came upon a ruined building that seemed strangely familiar to him. Unable to account for this, it suddenly flashed across his mind that this was the building described as the smugglers' retreat in Victor Hugo's 'Toilers of the Sea' which he had read years before. Later in the summer they had made an expedition to the island of Sark, so seldom visited by tourists. Here Tryon explored the remarkable caves of Sark during the low tides, in company with

47

a naturalist, and saw the sea anemones and interesting marine life of these caverns.

Tryon always remembered with amusement the local tradition of the drunkard's test, in returning from the island of Big Sark to Little Sark. 'In one place,' he writes, 'these islands are joined by a very narrow causeway. From the footpath across it the ground falls away abruptly to a drop of several hundred feet. A log lay at the town end of the causeway and if the drinker, returning home, could walk the log, it was safe for him to risk the narrow path. If not, he lay down to sleep where he was.'

'The second summer, 1878,' Tryon continues, 'we spent in Granville, Normandy, and Cancale, Brittany. Later we were in Venice, and part of a summer in Holland in the picturesque city of Dordrecht. Here I made many studies of the town and the endless marine life and scenery of the river Maas.' His picture, 'The River Maas,' dated 1881, now hangs in the collection of Tryon's work at Smith College and is one of his most notable marines of that period. Continuing, he says: 'I found here material quite to my taste and from it I painted a number of pictures. One of these "Dutch Boats in a Breeze," I exhibited at the Salon of 1881, where it was well hung and extensively noticed in the papers. In the same Salon, I also exhibited a larger picture called "Harvest in Normandy," and a water-color, "Windmills."'

During five years, then, Tryon worked in Paris in the winter and made sketching trips to the French coast in summer, or traveled in Italy, Holland, and other Continental countries. The effect of this rich European experience shows itself in his work in an increased knowledge of structure and anatomy, and

48

THE RIVER MAAS, DORDRECHT

a greater breadth of vision and in suppleness and fluency in the handling of pigment. Up to the time of his departure for Europe, his work was somewhat hard and tight, at least in his earlier pictures, as is characteristic of the work of many self-taught painters. His response to the varying moods of Nature had always showed in his work, but the pictures he sent home from Paris were freer and more loosely handled, with much more breadth and freshness. Not only was he quick to absorb what the schools could give him, but his visits to the great galleries were a revelation and stimulus to his mental and æsthetic perceptions and a cultivation of his taste. He made some beautiful copies in the Louvre, among them one of the head of Titian's 'Man with the Glove.' This copy is now owned by Smith College.

Tryon spoke often of the old masters in the Louvre, of Titian particularly, of Vermeer and the Dutchmen. Of the painters of France, Corot charmed him, Rousseau hardly less. Daubigny interested him in his student days, as he has said, in his later years not so much. Of all the European painting that he saw at this period none seems to have made a more lasting impression than the Giovanni Bellini in the Church of the Frari in Venice. He often said that this altar piece was, for him, perhaps the most beautiful picture in the world. The following letter addressed to me in Florence in 1897 contains a reference to it and is also interesting as showing his attitude toward travel:

'THE GAINSBOROUGH
226 WEST 59TH ST.
NEW YORK, *Feb.* 14, 1897

'Why, Edward! Methinks I hear a voice as of New England speaking from the effete cities of the Orient, a faint pipe of the

49

wanderer in foreign parts. A croak as of the bullfrog under the bush when the breath of Spring stirs his veins. The Pension Lucchesi stirs memories long dormant and even now of doubtful origin, possibly nothing more than "fromage gratin au croute." Had you reached Venice I could have sworn it was the odor of the lagoons at low tide, but as it came from Firenze, it must be the influence of the old masters.

'You are dead right in what you say about traveling in order to know better how to appreciate what we have at home, in your case not as necessary as to most persons, as I know you have always felt the value and charm of New England. As you say, one may travel long and never find the same or as fine a country as New England. And this is right; to the properly balanced mind the charm of one's native soil speaks a deeper language than any other. I doubt if by any but the landscape painter can this be quite understood, the effect of the subtle under-charm, the faint reminiscences of childhood days, the memories of many a day afield, and who shall not say that even pre-natal memories come in the form of intuitions too subtle to define and, often unconsciously transferred to the picture, are the saving note of all.

'But it is good to travel and see what man has done in the past, to store the mind with the riches of bygone times and thereby formulate a standard by which we may gauge the work of the present. One may feel timidly that we have as good scenery, as good art, as good a government as others, but there is nothing like testing for oneself the exact measure of difference....

'While you are in Venice don't fail to see the Bellini in the little room of the Church of the Frari, the Madonna with the

50

saints (I forget their trade-mark) on either side, a triptych, as I remember it something like this: [sketch] in lay-out, and to my mind the greatest piece of work in Venice. It is at times hard to get at it, as it (the church) is often closed and it takes some shekels to get it open....'

In addition to the pictures I have mentioned which influenced Tryon during his sojourn abroad, I remember others to which he called my attention when I began to study with him soon after his return home.

Many fine examples of contemporary French painting appeared in New York at this period, in exhibitions and sales. Among these Tryon praised the work of that distinguished still-life painter Vollon, and he described pictures by this artist which he had seen abroad, one in particular, a gorgeous rendering of a pumpkin reflected in a brass kettle. I recall a small reproduction of Bastien Lepage's portrait of his father which Tryon had in his studio, to which he directed the attention of his pupils as a fine piece of technique. The work of Cazin somewhat interested him, but he always said it fell short of greatness, possibly owing to the too long experience of Cazin as a decorator of porcelains, from the influence of which he never wholly escaped.

Though some of Tryon's youthful appraisals changed with his growth, the memories of the great masterpieces never faded. But I believe that Turner made the strongest impression upon him, in the field of landscape and marine painting. We have seen that, even at the age of twenty-one, Tryon was copying reproductions of Turner's pictures. Tryon told me, however, that at the time of his student life in Paris, his severely scien-

51

tific study of form somewhat blinded him to Turner's eminence, and for a time he did not hold this master in great esteem. As his tastes and sympathies broadened and his imagination quickened, he returned to the poetic visions of Turner. They enraptured him, and he never ceased, thenceforth, to love and admire them.

He often spoke of Turner's tremendous versatility and used to say, 'He has painted the whole visible world!' Tryon delighted to collect fine books that contained steel engravings of Turner's pictures, or that had been illustrated by him, like 'The Rivers of France' and Rogers's 'Poems.' These, in the early editions, contain examples of that greatest period of the art of steel engraving. The works represented are very beautiful and so marvelously delicate in execution that they appear magical.

Although by no means disparaging Thornbury's monumental work upon Turner's life, Tryon preferred Hamerton's biography, I think because the work was more condensed and also because it was written by a painter. Tryon, like some other artists, had a theory that artists in paint were better critics of painting than literary people. He also said of Hamerton's life of Turner, 'I don't like prefaces to books as a general thing, but the one in Hamerton's biography seems to me admirable.'

In the spring of 1925, about four months before Tryon's death, my son found, in New York, an exceptionally good set of colored reproductions of a large number of Turner's watercolors. When we went to call upon Tryon, we took them with us, thinking to divert his mind from his illness. He placed the portfolio upon a chair before him, and though so weak he could only look at a few at a time, he insisted upon going through the

52

entire collection, and dwelt long and lovingly upon each of the prints that he liked especially.

If a fine Turner came to New York and was on view at a dealer's, or in a private collection, Tryon made a point of seeing it. In the winter of 1925, two Turners from the Glenconner Collection were exhibited at Knoedler's Gallery. One of them was a large picture, 'Van Tromp's Shallop Entering the Scheldt.' There was a smaller one, too, a view of Venice. The latter picture aroused all of Tryon's admiration. He spoke in glowing terms of the rare charm of misty opalescent color in which the distant city hung, suspended between sea and sky. And he praised the quality of abstract creative vision which he felt in it.

In reading various works on Turner, I have been impressed repeatedly by a certain striking resemblance to Tryon. It has seemed to me that Tryon reincarnated much of the English painter, though he was a lyric, as Turner was an epic, poet. Born to somewhat the same conditions, and in physique and personal appearance strangely alike, the sturdy Briton and the shrewd New England Yankee had a vast deal in common in their characters, habits, and overpowering love of nature. Both were physically strong, vigorous, of great endurance. They loved the sea intensely, spent much time upon it, and were excellent sailors. Both were very fond of fishing, and combined it with their study of nature. Tryon's art was imbued with the spirit of a later age and, based upon a more rigorous interpretation of the facts of nature, was austere rather than exuberant, but both painters were preoccupied with analysis of color, atmospheric *nuances*, and complicated technical devices to enhance the charm and poetry of their pictures.

53

Studying their temperaments and noting so many points of likeness, it seems to me quite natural that Tryon should have been responsive to Turner's art, and that this artist should have been, to him, one of the greatest masters of landscape.

One trait of Tryon's, though of minor importance, was so akin to a well-known side of Turner's nature that I think it serves somewhat to bear out my contention. Both Thornbury and Hamerton, as well as other writers, have emphasized Turner's extreme frugality, carried often to the extent of parsimony, first exercised of necessity, afterward becoming the habit of his lifetime.

'William Turner, the barber,' says Hamerton, 'was a Devonshire man who had settled in London. His great characteristics appear to have been the especial virtues of the middle class, industry and economy. In teaching his son these things he helped in the artistic career itself, for without the most persistent industry the painter would never have mastered his art, and without the strictest economy in early years he would never have been able to pursue it with sufficient independence for the attainment of greatness. Thus William Turner gave his son both a sword and a shield for the battle of life, and if we were writing an allegory we might say that on the sword was engraven the word *Diligentia*, and on the shield *Parsimonia*.

'Few young men need these virtues so much as a young painter, for his art bristles all over with difficulties, and until fame is won he may be at any time compelled to abandon it from sheer necessity, against which there is no defense but thrift.'

The American also was born a poor boy. He passed through

54

a long period of early struggle and some hardship, and was obliged to exercise the strictest economy in order to live and paint. He thus formed the habits of frugality which persisted long after the necessity for them had passed. He was quite conscious of this and he often spoke humorously of it.

At Ogunquit on the Maine coast he appeared one morning carrying a pair of old shoes such as he wore when fishing or tramping the fields. With a smile he said to me: 'I have brought these shoes with me from home because I can get them tapped for a quarter by my old friend the cobbler across the way. I don't have to do this, but the habits of youth are so ingrained in me that I cannot wholly discard them.' He would pay thousands of dollars for a masterpiece of oil painting, or for expensive porcelains, potteries, and art objects for his home, and he always lived well, though simply, but he practiced many of the small economies throughout his life. Both Turner and Tryon were generous to a fault, however, in their hospitality, and their sympathetic help to those in trouble. And each of them left most of his fortune to the public for the uses of art.

At the end of five years of life abroad, or in the spring of 1881, Tryon felt that he had attained the object for which he went there. He had perfected himself in the technique of painting in the best schools in existence. He had cultivated his taste by study of the world's great masterpieces. And he had broadened his general culture and enriched his life by the years spent in one of the most highly civilized countries in Europe. Tryon always felt and expressed a profound respect for the French people, and acknowledged his debt to them for their influence upon his art. By this time, however, the money with which he and his wife started was nearly spent. He had sold some of the

55

pictures which he sent home from time to time, and he had eked out their resources by selling slight sketches in black and white to dealers in Paris, or for use as illustrations. But even with these and the frugal way in which they lived, he realized that he must turn again to making money.

'This same year,' he says, 'we decided to return to America, but before leaving Paris I must relate an incident which our friends said should be called "The Romance of the Poor Young Painter." On leaving America we had planned our finances so we felt we might be able to stay abroad for possibly a year and a half. We had already stayed nearly five years and our funds were at such a low ebb we were wondering where to turn for aid.

'Quite discouraged, I was wandering down the Rue Lafayette when in a window I saw a charming little picture by Corot. As I stood gazing at it, a gentleman stepped beside me and said in French, "A beautiful picture, is it not?"

'We conversed for a while, when he said, "Are you an artist and are you very familiar with the work of Corot?" I replied I was an admirer of his work and had studied it deeply. He then said he had recently purchased a Corot and asked me if I would be willing to give him my judgment upon it. This I readily agreed to, and together we went to his home on the Boulevard des Italiens. On an easel rested the picture in question, and at first glance I thought it a good example of the work of the master.

'As I studied it more carefully, doubt of its genuineness came to me. I then told him I considered it a spurious work and advised him to show it to M. Petit, a well-known expert. He asked for my card and promised to let me know the final decision.

'A few days later he called at my studio. He said the expert

56

agreed with my judgment on the picture. He then asked to see my work. Fortunately, I had four small pictures framed and ready to ship to New York for sale. These I showed him. He asked the price of each and, to my astonishment, said he would take them all. Thus by a miracle were we saved.'

If the reader is familiar with the habits of the average painter, he will know how seldom it is that an artist has even *one* of his finished pictures framed and ready for a chance showing. That Tryon had all four of his pictures framed was only another example of how, when Opportunity knocked at his door, he stood ready to welcome her.

VII

SOUTH DARTMOUTH

TRYON spent the first two summers following his return from
Europe, in 1881, at East Chester, then only a rural village comparatively remote from New York. He made sketches there
and painted a few pictures, not particularly characteristic or
significant, perhaps, though in one or two he struck an interesting note not often repeated. The subject of one of these that I
recall was a row of cottages underneath tall willows, with
figures of women hanging out washing. There were white ducks
and geese in a pool in the foreground, and the whole picture was
enveloped in the haze of a warm spring day. Delicate pinks
and greens prevailed in the color scheme.

Tryon did not find the character of East Chester very inspiring, and soon cast about for a summer home in more congenial surroundings. It was just at this time that his friend,
R. Swain Gifford, the landscape painter, called his attention to
the village of South Dartmouth, where we found Tryon at the
beginning of this book. Gifford himself had built a summer
cottage and studio at Nonquitt, two or three miles away.

SKETCH OF SOUTH DARTMOUTH

Tryon loved this village of his choice and eventually regarded it as his true and permanent home. New York was a temporary stopping-place only, a shelter from the winter's cold. He was wont to say, half in jest, that, did not the rigors of winter keep him indoors and drive him to painting, he doubted if he would do much work. Given a warmer climate and the freedom to sail, cruise, and fish, he feared his moral character would have given way entirely and his art have been neglected. He was extremely loath to leave the country in the fall and eager to return at the first hint of spring.

The country, the shore, and the sea about South Dartmouth and New Bedford have furnished inspiration and material for the major part of Tryon's work. They have the sturdiness and austerity that are typical of the landscape and coast of southern New England. The human element, also, of this Massachusetts hamlet influenced Tryon's art and contributed to his success. And no one who has not observed it can understand how, as the years passed, he took ever a deeper root among its people. As in the novels of Thomas Hardy, one breathes the peat smoke and treads the downs of Dorset, so Tryon's landscapes exhale native odors and stir emotions too elusive to transfix in words. I remember that Tryon once quoted George Moore as having said, 'No wonder Sarah Bernhardt could act love! She *was* love!' It seems to me a fair analogy to say of Tryon, 'No wonder he could paint New England! He *was* New England!'

The city of New Bedford in the early eighties had a population of forty to fifty thousand. The whaling industry, which reached its height between 1846 and 1850, and to which New Bedford had often contributed the largest fleet, had now dwindled from over five hundred ships to less than a hundred.

59

The whaling fleet of New England between 1877 and 1886 numbered about a hundred and fifty vessels, all told. There was, however, a sufficient number of whaleships bound out from and returning to New Bedford in 1884, and enough of the industry in evidence, to give the city and its outlying towns a decided spice of romance and adventure. One daily met and talked with men who might easily have furnished the *dramatis personæ* in Dana's 'Two Years Before the Mast' or Melville's 'Moby Dick.' Whaling permeated the village of South Dartmouth. Not only had whaleships been built there, but many of their most successful and noted captains and mates actually lived in the town, and, with their crews, formed a substantial fraction of its few hundred inhabitants. A grizzled sea-captain dwelt in every second or third house. Portuguese and Yankee boatsteerers shared the sidewalks with Grand Banks fishermen, mackerel catchers, lobstermen and clam-diggers. These, with their wives and families, gave a picturesque air to the little town that has long since passed away.

Padanaram consists of a main street about a mile long, shaded by fine old elms, and it runs north and south along the east shore of the Apponagansett River and Harbor. The village is bordered on the south by Buzzard's Bay. A few side streets and lanes intersect the principal thoroughfare, and the houses are mainly clustered about the water. Many of them, in the days in which this scene is laid, dated back to the early seventeenth century. They were beautiful examples of architecture, simple and dignified with delicately ornamented doorways and cornices. The smaller buildings, gray fish houses and boat shops, usually shingled all over, were relieved against a background of blue water. Dories and fishing boats, new or in advanced stages of decay, lobster pots, fish cars, nets, gear, and rusty anchors, filled the dooryards and contributed to the nautical air of the village.

Padanaram's unique industry of making salt by the evaporation of sea water, pumped from the bay by windmills into shallow wooden boxes or vats open to the sun, also added a truly salient feature to the landscape. The weather-beaten windmills and accessory low buildings, set upon flat marshes, decidedly suggested Holland.

Another object of local flavor was the covered hayrick — a stack of hay protected by a low pyramidal roof, supported by posts at the corners. I often sketched with Tryon near the outskirts of South Dartmouth, from 1885 to 1887, when these old red-roofed hayricks stood in almost every farmyard grouped with barns and outbuildings. He liked their severe simplicity, and they appear in a number of his early pictures as the dominant mass in the composition.

During the first few years of his residence at Padanaram, beginning about 1884, Tryon sketched and painted a good deal about the village itself, its streets and lanes, and the sheltered harbor. One picture in particular stands out in my memory which showed distinctly the result of his study abroad applied to a native subject. It measured about twenty by thirty inches, and for many years hung in the dining-room of his South Dartmouth home. The subject was a view of one of the streets of the village in summer. The roadway was bordered by old houses, their shingles mossy and silver gray. The graceful tower of the church rose above them, and daisies and wild flowers dotted the foreground. A man drove a couple of cows along the road, raising the dust as they walked, and over all the scene the heat of summer seemed to tremble and vibrate. This sentiment foreshadowed a future development of what might be called poetic realism in Tryon's more classic themes.

He painted a number of similar subjects of the village streets and lanes, often with figures, the old farmhouses and hayricks, the harbor and its boats, in these and the following years. They were always pleasing, but their interest lay mostly in a painter-like rendering of concrete and obvious facts. Surface qualities and the intrinsic pictorial value of the subject itself preoccupied him then more than subtle suggestiveness or the interpretation of the lyric poetry of Nature's shyer moods which hold so great a place in his later work.

Tryon soon began, however, to explore and paint the country more remote from the village. Across the river and bay to the west and two or three miles distant from his house lay a sequestered bit of country as typical of rural New England as could anywhere be found. The few scattered farms that lay adjacent to its borders scarcely encroached on its wild seclusion and only enhanced its virginal charm.

Great oaks grew here that might well have served Rousseau for *motifs* in the Forest of Fontainebleau. Groves of white birches, graceful and delicate, surrounded and partially veiled them. The earth, roughly level, was undulating, and granite ledges cropped out everywhere, with glacial boulders scattered thickly in abandoned pastures, long grown up and choked by fragrant bayberry, sweet fern, and huckleberry bushes. They were a fit covering, an embroidered garment for this rugged and sinewy embodiment of primeval nature. Old stone walls, half fallen down, emphasized the bold modeling of the ground and gave the one faint suggestion of humanity.

DARTMOUTH MOORLANDS

'Oh, good gigantic smile o' the brown old earth,
   This autumn morning! How he sets his bones
To bask i' the sun, and thrusts out knees and feet
   For the ripple to run over in its mirth;
Listening the while, where on the heap of stones
   The white breast of the sea-lark twitters sweet.' [1]

Given the rich color of late October and early November, when the deciduous trees have dropped their leaves, when the oaks are reddish bronze, the birches golden and the bushes scarlet, the stage was set for the artist who had wandered hither. The beauty of it was bewildering. Forcing one's way through a tangled thicket of bull brier and blackberry runners, one emerged to face a classic landscape of russet oaks and slender birches with sparkling notes of red in the bushes and silver in the rocks. A few steps more to a clearing and a noble moorland stretched away, simple and austere, with granite ledges in the nearer foreground. A rutted cart-path wound among the rocks and underbrush, and led on to a low white farmhouse with a wisp of smoke blowing from its chimney. On the far horizon South Dartmouth nestled along its side hill in tiny dots of gray and white, above the blue waters of the bay. Here was material admirably suited to Tryon's genius, ready to his hand, which he quickly made his own.

He painted a fine landscape, inspired by such a scene as I have described, in his New York studio, I think during the first winter that I studied there, in 1885. This large canvas, thirty-one by fifty-two inches, called 'Dartmouth Moorlands,' now hangs in the collection of Tryon's work at Smith College.

In a letter written to Miss Beulah Strong, his assistant there in the Art Department, he says: 'This picture was painted

[1] From Robert Browning's 'Among the Rocks.'

directly, not from nature, but from a small study. The only special quality that differentiates it from others is that a wax medium was used. It was painted *premier coup* throughout.'[1] It must have been executed in a very short time, probably in a couple of days, for when I left his studio at the end of a lesson the bare canvas stood upon his easel, and upon returning after an interval of four or five days, I was surprised to see the completed picture.

Standing before this landscape one involuntarily draws a deep breath of exhilaration, as if in the presence of Nature herself. The very spirit of an autumn afternoon is in its spacious and breezy freshness. As the westering sun drops lower, in its parting glance, and the shadow in the foreground creeps forward, how the distant bit of country, in its garment of pale green and russet reds, glows and sparkles! One can readily understand why this picture was loudly applauded when it came before the jury of the Society of American Artists, where it was exhibited the following spring.

During Tryon's first summers at Padanaram, before he built his own boat, he sailed and fished a great deal in the smack of Captain West, a local market fisherman. After a day's work in the bay, they disposed of their catch at a New Bedford wharf and then ran over to Fair Haven and anchored for the night. It was while lying outside of Crow Island in New Bedford Harbor on this fishing boat that Tryon came on deck one morning to see a beautiful sunrise over the little town of Fair Haven. The sky was suffused with golden films of cloud, repeated in lower tone in the water, the lights in the houses and streets not yet extinguished. The square tower of the church rose above

[1] *Bulletin* of Smith College Museum, March 30, 1924.

64

DAYBREAK, FAIRHAVEN, NEW BEDFORD HARBOR

the central group of buildings, a few boats rode at anchor, and a waning moon paled in the morning sky. Tryon was using the loft of an old barn for a studio at this time, and a day or two after he saw this effect of dawn, a completed and charming picture of it greeted my eyes as I climbed the stairs. This work took a prize at the galleries of the American Art Association the following winter and, after different ownerships, now hangs in the collection of the Rhode Island School of Design in Providence.

Many of Tryon's best pictures of this period were painted from memory, with few data other than hasty sketches of lead pencil on the back of an envelope or scrap of paper. Even when he sailed and fished, his sensitive mind and memory retained Nature's moving panorama like a photographic film. With an inexorable grip of the material facts, he could paint the spirit of a transitory effect and clothe it with convincing reality. He used to say that it was much easier to remember the color than the form, and he generally jotted down a few stenographic notes of the big masses, relations, or design, in the glimpses of passing scenery.

Curiously, he never seemed very well prepared with any materials to make even these slight notes, though he could sometimes fish out the half-inch stub of a lead pencil from his pocket. Often when sailing, walking the fields, or riding together in a railway train, he would turn to me and say, 'Have you a pencil and a bit of paper?' Supplied with what was necessary, he usually filled a space about the size of a visiting-card with what looked to be crude and undecipherable hieroglyphics, quite like writing in shorthand. He did, however, sometimes carry water-colors and sketch-pad, and occasionally completed a pencil drawing with washes of color. His friend George Alfred Williams, the artist, designed and gave him a very small and compact water-color box. Tryon was greatly pleased with this vest-pocket convenience, and made with it a series of tiny water-colors. Most of them were marines of the coast at Ogunquit.

Tryon's life upon the water in summer naturally afforded constant provocation to record changing effects of sea and sky. As often as not he showed no outward sign of receiving a mental impression, nor did he make any visible notation. On one of the first cruises in his boat, we lay in Newport Harbor for a few days where we had gone to see the cup races. In the dark of night Tryon stood in the companionway of the sloop looking at the brilliant spectacle. There were hundreds of yachts at anchor, their riding lights set, and the soft, rich glow of portholes and cabin windows and the sharper electric lights of the city in the background, all reflected in the water. He commented upon the sparkling fairylike radiance of the scene. Then we went below and turned in. Soon after our return to South Dartmouth a day or two later, he painted this nocturne from memory. He called it 'Newport at Night.' It is in the collection of Burton Mansfield, of New Haven.

What I have written I think will show that Tryon found congenial surroundings in South Dartmouth and its environs. It was decidedly an example of love at first sight. Spiritually and physically he had discovered his *milieu*, a mine of wealth in subject material that no lifetime could exhaust. Not only did the romantic and colorful landscape inspire him to paint, but the alluring playground that, with the sea, it afforded for his recreation could not have been more to his taste. The

66

NEWPORT AT NIGHT

natives, too, were of kindred blood with him, hardy seafaring people, simple in their lives, industrious, courageous, and with a generous sprinkling of odd and amusing characters, to render life among them zestful and entertaining. Tryon and his new neighbors felt their consanguinity at the start. Often their acquaintance ripened into friendships. From prosperous sea-captains retired from service and settled comfortably in the village, to the local cranks and oddities of the human species who abounded in country towns of that time, Tryon soon had a wide range of acquaintance, and he added to it as the years went on. To walk along the village street with him was to hear cordial greetings on all sides. Hands were waved, sailors and fishermen hailed him from boat shop and wharf. He stopped to chat with the village blacksmith, and if a lobsterman was haul-ing out his boat, Tryon lent a helping hand.

On the way to the remote section of the South Dartmouth country I have described lay a mile or more of marshland, partially dry and full of interesting subjects, with its patches of brown sand, tall rushes and mallows, and pools where herons stalked. In the middle of this plain there lived a hermit in an age-old house of the seventeenth century. He was the last of his race, and no woman or child had ever broken or changed his course of life, or ruffled the serenity of his retirement from the world. His house was almost literally filled to its cubic capac-ity with every conceivable relic. There were not only seafaring and farming implements, but, in the conglomerate mass of ancient fishing gear, whaling lances, harpoons, harnesses, and logging chains, there lurked a choice piece of antique furniture of the colonial days. The hermit did not encourage callers; in fact, access to the house was difficult. For days at a time the

67

only sign of life about the old building was a thin feather of smoke from its massive chimney. The place was a bit uncanny. Children shunned it. Tryon, however, in his rambles had penetrated the old man's reserve, and together we often sat upon the doorstep of this strange dwelling and listened to the vagaries of a soul so secluded that he might have been a visitor from another planet. Tryon had a genius for exploring such natures. They had been familiar to him from boyhood, and they responded to him sympathetically. From the amazing mass of junk which filled the home of this recluse Tryon extricated a highboy of solid rosewood, beautifully proportioned, which the old man readily sold to him. It stood in his bedchamber until his death as a cabinet for his fishing-reels, bass and trout flies, and delicate tackle.

Country people delighted Tryon. Unlike many artists and literary folk who are wont to be intolerant of provinciality and of those who do not share their own intellectual interests, Tryon never quarreled with or felt superior to humble people. The pungent flavor of rural life was akin to the spirit of his pictures. He loved whatever smacked of the soil, of the hard labor of a scanty living, wrested with difficulty from barren and unfruitful land. He always lingered to talk with the natives, farmers and fishermen, and his rich store of anecdotes of them was very diverting.

The farms about South Dartmouth did not yield a generous living to their owners. The soil was poor, and even after the land had been cleared and the stone walls built, the fields were still studded with a superabundance of drift boulders, valuable for landscape foregrounds, but not helpful in ploughing a straight furrow. In one of these rough old pastures one autumn,

Tryon was sketching near a farmhouse, when its owner approached. After inspecting the sketch, the farmer complained of his difficulties in making a living from the infertile soil and said he was much discouraged. 'In fact,' he said, 'I had hard work this year to make both ends meet.' Tryon condoled with him and said he well understood the barrenness of the country and how hard it must be to make farming pay. 'However,' he said, 'it yields me a pretty good crop. I took fifteen hundred dollars from your farm alone last year.' 'The devil you did!' said the man in amazement. 'What do you mean?' 'Well,' said Tryon, 'do you remember the sketch you saw me making near here last fall?' 'I do,' replied the farmer — 'what of it?' 'Why,' answered Tryon, 'I painted a picture in New York last winter from that sketch and sold it for fifteen hundred dollars.' 'Good God!' exclaimed the farmer. 'I'd 'a' sold ye the whole farm for that much money!'

On another occasion Tryon had painted a picture called 'The Haystack,' and one of his patrons had the purchase of it under consideration, when Tryon, the spring having come, left New York for the country. Shortly after his arrival at South Dartmouth the postmaster received a telegram for him which ran as follows: 'Will buy Haystack for five hundred dollars. Signed ——' With the usual tendency of interesting news to filter quickly through a rural community, by the time Tryon landed from his boat at evening he was beset on all sides by farmers and villagers anxious to know when and where he had sold a haystack at such a record-breaking price.

'Oh! the beautiful chestnut-colored cow standing up to the belly in the marshy grass,' said Corot. '...It is adorable — I will paint it — Crack! there it is, splendid, splendid; goodness, how striking it is! Let us see what this peasant will say who stands watching me paint, but is too shy to approach. "I say there, Simon!" Good! Here is Simon, approaching and looking. "Well, Simon, what do you think of that?" "Oh, really, sir, it is very beautiful!" "And do you see what I wish to represent?" "I think I see what it is; it is a large yellow rock you have placed there!"" [1]

Tryon enjoyed criticism of this kind as much as the great Frenchman. An old lady drew near as he was sketching at Rocky Hill one spring, on the banks of the Connecticut. Peering at the sketch, she said in a querulous tone, 'Are ye drawin' off the river?' Again, a farmer discovered Tryon in his orchard painting the apple trees in blossom. He hastened up, scowling, and snarled aggressively, 'I shan't buy it!' 'You couldn't,' returned Tryon; 'you haven't money enough!'

Before long the people of South Dartmouth considered Tryon as one of themselves. They not only liked him as a man, but they came to value and reverence his art, in so far as they understood it; and they were very proud of his reputation which was eventually so closely associated with the town and its inhabitants. In truth, no man could have been better liked or more respected by his neighbors than was Tryon in his adopted home.

As the years went by, the charming old country village changed imperceptibly but steadily. With the increase of population and wealth of New Bedford, whose cotton mills have made it again a prosperous and busy city, it was impossible that the attractions of South Dartmouth as a summer resort should be overlooked. The old farms were bought by wealthy

[1] David Croal Thomson: *The Barbizon School.* Scribner's, 1890.

people who built pretentious mansions along the harbor and, denuding the unkempt pastures of rocks, bushes, and native growths, transformed them into sleek lawns and formal gardens. The laboring people of the city also, the Portuguese and French Canadians, workers in the mills, overran Padanaram and dotted its shores with bungalows and shacks. Tryon sat by, a rather sad but philosophic observer of the blighting effect of the Philistine mind upon his erstwhile Paradise.

He had seen trolley cars replace the old stagecoach that used to ply once a day from the village to the city. Then, from about 1904 to the present, an ever-increasing procession of automobiles pounded back and forth over the old bridge near his house, and added the noise of their horns to the broadcasting of a large radio station at Nonquitt. We sat together on his veranda one summer evening, some twenty years ago. The transformation was well under way and he saw with intuition the handwriting on the wall. 'I am glad,' said he, 'that I have lived my life when I did. My lines have been cast in pleasant places. I am thankful that I shall not be alive a hundred years from now. There are too many people in the world, and, for the most part, they do not know what to do with it.'

Still, such was his cheerfulness of mind, he did not allow the desecration of his beloved *campagna* to depress him or mar his enjoyment of nature. The sea was still his, secure in its unspoiled freshness, and by going a little farther afield, he could find most of his Forest of Fontainebleau unpolluted by motors, radios, or aeroplanes, even though his Ville d'Avray was invaded.

Tryon's philosophy ever served and saved him. He wasted no time on futile regrets at humanity's antics and devastations, but when the world was too much with him, quietly withdrew a little farther into his solitudes. Nothing daunted or disturbed him very much. As I was always curious of his response to different writers, I once asked him his opinion of La Rochefoucauld, knowing his interest in French literature. 'Well,' he said, 'I don't care very much for him; he is clever, but I am too much of an optimist to stomach his cynicism.' He found Emerson most inspiring, in his serene and noble philosophy. Emerson and Thoreau were two of his favorite authors. In fact, Tryon met the encroachments of a materialistic and mechanical age more than halfway. Instead of being soured by them, he gladly made the acquaintance of newcomers when he found them congenial. He joined the New Bedford Yacht Club, which had, in the later years, selected South Dartmouth as its summer station, and erected a clubhouse there. He took an active part in the Club's events and he was always in demand to serve on the race committees.

Never having had a child of his own, he took an especial interest in the children of the summer residents. He taught them to sail and fish, and often supplied them with tackle of his own manufacture. Sometimes when any of these young people showed a talent for art or literature, Tryon became their mentor and guided their footsteps with all of a father's care and solicitude. He always enjoyed contact with young minds and found them stimulating. So he lived on at South Dartmouth, adjusting himself somewhat to the changes of time, but still following closely the habits of his youth. Summer after summer he spent in complete surrender to the happiness of a healthy physical existence, while his mind stored itself afresh with new impressions of nature, new impulses to creative work. In one

72

sense it was an uneventful life, but it was also rich and full of happenings significant to the artist.

In looking over some of Tryon's papers after his death, I found in an old diary the following quotation from Matthew Arnold:

'We cannot kindle when we will
The fire which in the heart resides,
The spirit bloweth and is still,
In mystery our soul abides.
But tasks in hours of insight willed
Can be through hours of gloom fulfilled.'

VIII

TRYON IN NEW YORK

We must now go back to the time of Tryon's return from Europe, in the spring of 1881. Soon after his arrival he took a studio in the Rembrandt Building in West Fifty-Seventh Street in New York. He had for neighbors in the building Thomas W. Dewing, William Bailey Faxon, Will H. Low, R. Swain Gifford, William Sartain, George Wharton Edwards, and Joe Jefferson, who liked to think his landscapes were as good as his acting.

Tryon had now been gone from home five years, so long that he had lost touch with former purchasers of his pictures, and, as he had not had time to establish a new clientèle, he turned again to teaching to assure himself a small but dependable income. For this he was now admirably equipped by his study abroad, and he soon formed a small class of pupils who drew and painted two days a week in his studio, leaving him the remaining time for his own work.

His painting, in the interval of his absence, had been in a transition period, changing from his early moods and manners to the first indications of his future style.

74

The quality and interest of his pictures, however, soon began to appeal again, not only to the connoisseur and collector, but to the taste of people who had an instinct for beauty. He had not been painting long before he formed acquaintances among the patrons of art in New York and elsewhere, and when spring came his pictures of the preceding winter were usually sold, either from his studio or from exhibitions. It was seldom that he had even one work on hand when he left New York for the country.

In the year 1878, a short time before Tryon's return from Europe, N. E. Montross began to show a few pictures by American artists in a narrow hallway adjoining his store at 1380 Broadway. This venture was the beginning of the future Montross Art Galleries, the first of which was established at 372 Fifth Avenue in 1900, the second at 550 Fifth Avenue in 1910, and the present one in East Fifty-Sixth Street in 1925. In this small room, lighted by a window at one end, Mr. Montross showed from time to time a landscape by Tryon or J. Francis Murphy, a figure picture by Dewing, or, perhaps, a small bronze by Phimister Proctor.

These artists, with the gradual addition of a few others like A. P. Ryder, John La Farge, Horatio Walker, and Alexander Schilling, formed the nucleus of that select company which, for the ensuing twenty-five years, made Montross exhibitions notable in New York. The pictures were few, but choice in quality. Tryon and Dewing were constant contributors.

Among the first pictures that Tryon exhibited in Montross's small room was a spring landscape. Tryon said of it: 'I had sacrificed nearly everything to secure a certain quality of light of the early morning, a delicate effect suggestive of cobwebs

75

and dew on the grass. One day I was in the store and Montross said to me, "I had a call from a painter the other day who made what seemed to me a very significant remark about your picture." I asked what it was and Montross replied, "He said, 'That picture is a sacrifice of the things that are not for the things that are.'" I said, "Well, the man who said that is a thinker. He has a head and can use it. Who is he?" "Homer Martin," answered Montross. After that I met Homer Martin and told him how much I appreciated his comment. We saw each other frequently thereafter at the Century Club, where we often played a game of billiards, or talked of painting....'

Thomas B. Clarke, the collector, began to buy paintings in the early eighties. Tryon's landscapes attracted his attention. He visited the studio frequently and purchased pictures. Clarke at this time was also acquiring his first fine group of landscapes by George Inness, and his house was so crowded, from entrance hall to attic, with these and other paintings that it was difficult to see them for lack of good light. Among Tryon's pictures, Clarke bought a number of his early moonlights. In one of them there is the figure of a man driving a flock of sheep homeward at night. Tryon introduced figures in his pictures less often, however, as he advanced, until in his later works they seldom appear. He used to say that the worse the painting of figures was, in landscape, the better the effect, and I think he ended by feeling them, or anything but a faint suggestion of them, to be an intrusion, at least in his own landscapes.

In the year 1889, Tryon first met Charles L. Freer, the connoisseur and collector. This meeting was an important event in Tryon's art life. Mr. Freer, whose history reads like a romance, started in life as a poor boy in the Middle West, and, after many vicissitudes and hardships, achieved a phenomenal success in business. He and his friend, Colonel Frank J. Hecker, worked first on a small railroad as train hands. They later went to Detroit, and, with a few thousand dollars they had saved, began to build railroad cars. This business prospered enormously and they eventually sold out their interest in it at a profit of several million dollars each. Banking and other enterprises added to Mr. Freer's fortune, but he had, along with his business activities and successes, for many years developed an interest in art. He eventually devoted practically all of his time to it and formed the invaluable collection that is housed in the gallery in Washington which he built and gave to the Nation and which bears his name. I will quote Tryon's words describing briefly the circumstances of their first meeting:

'... My acquaintance with Mr. Freer began in the year 1889 when he purchased from me a picture I had just completed, "The Rising Moon." This picture he told me was the first oil painting he had bought. He had previously purchased several water-colors and had been for some years a collector of etchings and prints. Even at that early date, his collection of Whistler's etchings was quite extensive. The picture "The Rising Moon," which he first bought of me, has an amusing history. A few days after its completion, I had a call from Mr. Potter Palmer, of Chicago. He saw the picture and liked it, and later brought Mrs. Palmer to see it. They both agreed they would like the picture, but said, as they were sailing for Europe the next day, they would wait until their return before making a final decision. I suggested that if they wanted it they had better engage it, as it might not remain with me long. Soon after that the picture became the property of Mr. Freer.

'The following summer the Chicago Art Institute held an exhibition which was to a certain extent international. I was asked to contribute a picture and Mr. Freer kindly allowed me to show "The Rising Moon." The principal prize in this exhibition was one of one thousand dollars, given by Potter Palmer. This prize was awarded to my picture.

'Soon after my return in the autumn to my New York studio, Mr. and Mrs. Potter Palmer called, as they said, to get their picture. They seemed much annoyed when told that it was sold. I gave them no hint of its destination, and it was only after their arrival in Chicago that they learned of its fate.

'To the International Exposition held in Munich in 1892, this picture was again loaned by Mr. Freer. It was there awarded the gold medal of the first class. This picture now rests with many of my later works in the Freer Gallery in Washington, D.C....'

Tryon's acquaintance with Freer ripened into a warm friendship which lasted until Freer's death. With the latent qualities of a great connoisseur, Freer now rapidly developed his taste and appreciation by a serious and exhaustive study of art in its largest aspect and remotest origins. He sought the sources of the plastic arts and delved deeply into them with the intelligence of a student and scholar, combined with the enterprise of a successful business man. Not satisfied with the superficial phases of the contemporary painting of his native country, he organized expeditions of his own and journeyed to remote and little-known regions of China, Japan, Ceylon, and Korea, to ancient temples and shrines where the matchless art of those

THE RISING MOON

civilizations had its birth. He pursued beauty by sea and land, all over the world. Chinese pirates attacked his boats on the inland rivers of Mongolia, fevers and miasma threatened his life in the steaming rice-fields of China, but he was indomitable. The sacred temples yielded their precious spoil to him in bronze and marble Buddhas; ink paintings by priests or wondrously beautiful carvings. He ransacked the Chinese and Japanese cities and obtained access to the choicest examples of their ancient art. He was intimate with the collectors and art dealers of these Oriental capitals. He knew and entertained at his home in Detroit the curators of some of Europe's finest museums, and to their amazement he sometimes showed them finer examples of Rakka pottery or Chinese porcelain and jade than their own collections could boast. Dr. Bode, of the Berlin Museum, was one of these who once told Freer with pride of a rare piece of Rakka the Museum owned which the learned expert considered the finest he knew.

As they made their way through Freer's collection in his Detroit house, Freer casually brought forth a Rakka jar which caused Bode to exclaim, 'Why, that is finer than ours in the Berlin Museum!'

Freer smiled and said quietly, 'I have six more as good or better than that!'

Along with Freer's absorbing interest in the study of the history of art and coincident with his world-wide search for works of other races and older civilizations, then accessible, now no longer obtainable, he maintained a lively interest in the best of contemporary art. The longer he studied the ancients and extended his knowledge, the more severely critical he became and the more refined his taste.

Surveying the field of oil painting in the eighties and nine-
ties, its best tendencies seemed to him exemplified in the art of
James McNeill Whistler abroad, and of Thomas W. Dewing,
Abbott H. Thayer, and Dwight W. Tryon in this country. He
believed the best traditions, the most spiritual and abstract
qualities of all that had gone before were perpetuated in the
painting of these men. He felt that they, of all our artists,
sought and captured the purest beauty, upheld the dignity of
the greatest periods, breathed the utmost refinement and exercised the most exquisite taste. Accordingly, Freer acquired
their work systematically, to round out and complete his
great collection.

Freer began to call regularly upon Whistler during trips
abroad, became his friend and purchased many of Whistler's
finest works, paintings in oil and water-color, pastels, etchings,
and lithographs. Tryon and Dewing, who were in close touch
with Freer during these years, knew the accessions to his collection of other than their own works, and they often counseled
with and advised him. Learning that the famous 'Peacock
Room' or dining-hall in Leyland's house in London, decorated
by Whistler, was for sale, a fact not then generally known in
England, Freer went to Tryon and said, 'The "Peacock Room"
in London is for sale and I can buy it. Would you get it, and
what do you think of the price asked?' Tryon replied in substance as follows: 'You already have a very important part of
Whistler's work, a great deal of the best of it. The "Peacock
Room" shows Whistler in one of his best phases, that of a
decorator. It is one of his distinguished things. The price is
comparatively low, and I think you ought to have it.'

There was a project in England at this time to have the

Government or private individuals buy the 'Peacock Room' for a public gallery, but before this could be carried out, Freer sailed for England, quietly negotiated for and bought it at sixty-three thousand dollars, and was at home before the English people knew what had happened. When they found out, it caused a commotion and considerable discomfiture in art circles.

Though Freer's restriction of his patronage of contemporary art to the work of the four artists he selected has doubtless seemed to many too exclusive and neglectful of much that was excellent in American art at that time, he was not unmindful of other contemporary painting. Along with his groups of pictures by Whistler, Dewing, Tryon, and Thayer, he also formed a smaller collection of about one hundred works by such American artists as he considered most representative of our native art in general. Among them are Brush, Sargent, Ryder, Winslow Homer, Hassam, and Metcalf. They are now included in the collection of the Freer Gallery.

Freer built a house in Detroit designed for him by Wilson Eyre, to contain his rapidly growing collection of art objects. He invited Dewing and Tryon to decorate certain rooms in it. In the little reception room at the left of the entrance, Dewing evolved an opalescent, shimmering dream of color and pattern, comparable to a peacock's breast or the wings of a butterfly. In an arching panel over the mantel he painted a decorative portrait of his daughter as a child, holding two kittens in her arms, which fitted delightfully into the general harmony. On a pedestal in the room a small statuette by MacMonnies added a kindred accent of elegance, and the furniture and hangings completed its unity.

Tryon thus notes his own part in the decoration: 'When Mr. Freer built his house in Detroit, I was commissioned to paint a series of decorations for the large hall which occupied the center of it. There were four wall spaces and two overmantels. For the small spaces I painted the four seasons, the "Springtime" filling the largest space. Over the mantels were "Dawn" and "Evening." These pictures are now in the Freer Gallery in Washington....'

One of these decorations of Tryon's, the 'Winter,' was a long panel, severely simple in its flat plane of snow-covered hillside against the fading light of evening, and filled with the chill spirit of the season. Tryon related with amusement Dewing's response to the austerity of this picture. When Dewing first saw it, he exclaimed in his sardonic way, 'A thousand miles from home and friends all dead!'

In a letter to his friend, George Alfred Williams, the artist, Tryon also refers to the decorations:

'I want to say a few words regarding the pictures you refer specially to. They are all a more or less conscious effort to produce rhythm of emotion when applied to decoration. They are the offspring of the large hall decorations for Freer's house.

'The room they were in was very simple, classic, severe in fact, and as Freer's taste corresponded, I tried, in a series of four pictures which filled all the four walls (and represented the four seasons) to make the paintings an integral part of the room and carry out, as far as possible, the classic purity of the design. For this reason I kept the flat horizon lines in the four panels of the same height. The horizontal lines of the ground, supplemented and offset by the verticals in the trees, seemed to make them a part of the architecture of the room.

82

'I think all who saw the room felt that, in a mysterious way, the pictures fitted and completed the whole thing. After spending so much time as I did on this theme (two years), it was natural for me to try to embody the idea in isolated easel pictures, hence came the long "Dawn" and a number of other similar works. I think they are quite my own and unlike the work of any other man....'

Tryon, in describing to me how he had treated the walls of Freer's hall to harmonize with his murals, said that he had painted the decorations against the low-toned tapestry background of his studio, and, although they were very high in key, in fact so high that the darkest shadow in some of them was a delicate purple, yet, when they were in place in Freer's house, they did not seem right with the light-toned colors around them. So he had a house-painter cover the inside of the room and ceiling with Dutch metal, red or copper below and silver above; then he took Vandyke brown and Antwerp blue and spotted it on the side walls in irregular patches of each color, of just the right consistency and fluidity to work well, and then, taking a big brush, he worked and blended it over the Dutch metal. He said the interior of the room, after the Dutch metal was on, looked like a brass kettle. He then used cobalt blue on the ceiling in the same way. He remarked to Freer, beforehand, that so much Dutch metal might be expensive, but Freer said, 'Go ahead! Do as you like!'

The walls, when completed, were ideal as backgrounds, keeping their place, subordinate to the decorations, and yet glowing with a quiet richness, handsome in color themselves.

In 1904, Freer took abroad with him a wood engraving, by Eldridge Kingsley, of the large decoration, 'Springtime,' and

83

showed it to Whistler. In a letter to Tryon, written on ship-board, *en route* to Ceylon, he says, in a postscript, ' ... This is to tell you that Whistler was delighted with the engraving of "Springtime." I took him the impression you selected and marked for him. He bade me thank both yourself and Kings-ley. The technical qualities of the printing, engraving, and, of course, the whole thing, in fact, rather puzzled him. He de-clared it refreshing and modern and charming.'

From the first year of their acquaintance Freer constantly purchased much of Tryon's most important work, along with that of the other three artists of his choice. Indeed, his yearly acquisition of Tryon's masterpieces became so habitual that after several years Freer felt that perhaps he was monopolizing Tryon's output to the disadvantage of other collectors and the picture-buying public. He told Tryon that, since he had al-ready a very representative group of his work, he would stop buying for a certain period, that others might have a chance at them, for, as Freer remarked, 'I do not like to have it said that I am the only person who can get a picture from Tryon.' He did not wholly cease, however, and in the interval he acquired a series of Tryon's most successful pastels — varied moods of the sea, inspired by the Maine coast at Ogunquit.

Freer continued to collect in the Oriental countries until the failure of his health, which was possibly due to the hard-ships he endured on some of his expeditions.

During the latter part of his life, Freer was much restricted in his diet. He nevertheless enjoyed entertaining his friends. I called upon Tryon rather late one evening in New York, and arrived just as he returned from the Plaza, where he had been dining with Freer. Though Tryon was usually most abstemi-

84

ous in his eating and drinking, I thought I detected a note of more than his usual cheerfulness, a noticeable air of well-being and satisfaction with the world. I said, 'It seems needless to ask you how you are; you evidently feel in the best of health and spirits.' He smilingly replied, 'Well, why shouldn't I? I've just had dinner with Freer. He had bread and milk, and I started with a cocktail and followed it with sherry, sauterne, and champagne with their respective courses, and liqueurs after the dessert. No wonder I'm cheerful!' A rare indulgence for Tryon, who was one of the most temperate of men.

The two friends kept in touch with each other during Freer's absence abroad, and his letters to Tryon are extremely interesting, not only in their accounts of his extensive travels, adventures, and researches in the world's most alluring treasure-houses of art, but because they so clearly indicate his character and charming personality.

While Tryon and Dewing admired each other's work unreservedly and were in the utmost sympathy, they, like most artists, had favorite painters, pet theories, and a bias for or against certain styles in art. As one might infer from the extreme elegance and fragility of the women in Dewing's pictures, he did not care greatly for the sturdy peasants of Millet and their homely clumsiness. Tryon, on the contrary, found something wholesome and vigorous about them, and the fact that they reeked of the soil was to him an attraction. Knowing their difference of opinion about Millet, Freer took a mischievous pleasure in stirring up discussions between his two artist friends, Dewing and Tryon, when they visited him together. Tryon relates how Freer used artfully to insinuate the subject

85

into the conversation at dinner. '... Dewing pitched into old Millet, but I defended him, and we went at it, hammer and tongs, while Freer sat back and enjoyed the circus immensely.'

Nothing gave Freer more pleasure than to go through the house with an appreciative friend and dwell long and lovingly upon the triumphs of painter or sculptor of modern time or of the ancient world. Tryon told me of visits to Freer which were, as he expressed it, 'artistic debauches.' For two or three days in succession, starting after breakfast, entering a favorably lighted room or gallery they would study potteries and porcelains, paintings, carvings or textiles of the great periods, brought to them by Stephen, Freer's trained manservant, until, forgetful of the lapse of time, the end of the day found them surfeited and weary. They rested for a day or two, then continued their excursions until they could hold no more.

It may seem rather strange that two men, whose lives, in some ways, were so strongly contrasted, were drawn as closely together as Tryon and Freer. It is true that they were both what is called 'self-made.' They had similar experiences in the hardships and struggles of their early lives. But Freer, when he had achieved success and acquired wealth, became a very sophisticated man of the world, a cosmopolite. He consorted with all sorts and conditions of men in many countries. He was a man of large affairs; his outlook on life was wide. Tryon, on the other hand, always remained somewhat provincial. His visits to Freer in Detroit took him farther away from home than he usually went. For years he simply alternated between New York and South Dartmouth with great regularity. His painting and his fishing occupied him to the exclusion of pretty

86

much everything else. But he and Freer had one bond in common, the quest for beauty. It drew them closely together from their first meeting. And it was the ruling passion of both to the very end of their lives.

IX

THE TEACHER — SMITH COLLEGE

We HAVE seen that Tryon, upon his return from Europe in 1881, took a private class in drawing and painting in his New York studio during the winter. The enthusiasm of his pupils for his instructions brought him to the attention of college presidents and others who tried to engage his services as a teacher of art. The trustees of one of our leading universities held several conferences with him with a view to his employment, but without result, as Tryon insisted that, if he were given charge, the course in art would have to be made an integral part of the curriculum and not an unimportant elective. He held broad views upon the subject of teaching, and considered the cultural side of the study of painting of equal importance with its technique. These theories were too radical for the average college president, who knew little of art and was inclined to regard it as a minor adjunct of education.

President L. Clark Seelye, of Smith College, however, was an exception. Tryon used to say that, while the natives of the New England of his time were mostly cold and unresponsive to æsthetic influences, Nature occasionally rebelled, and an otherwise austere soul, breaking the bonds of conformity and convention, would find delight in the genial atmosphere of the fine arts. If this theory needs confirmation, I am sure William Morris Hunt's experience with some of the Bostonians of his time in 1870 amply verifies it. President Seelye had high ideals of the education of women. He stood almost alone among college officials in recognizing the cultural value of art and music and the importance of their influence upon future wives and mothers, to say nothing of the refining effect, by association, upon the men they married.

This was demonstrated more than once by the encouragement to art by the husbands of Smith College graduates. A woman, who as a young girl had painted with Tryon at Smith College and assimilated the lessons of culture taught by the College art collections, so interested her husband in these things that he built and endowed the beautiful Albright Gallery in Buffalo.

Through one of Tryon's private pupils his reputation as a teacher had become known to President Seelye, who for two or three years, though without success, tried to persuade Tryon to take the position of instructor in art at Smith. J. Wells Champney became the first teacher of drawing at the College, to be succeeded by J. H. Niemeyer, afterwards professor at the Yale School of Fine Arts. Finally in 1885, after considerable negotiation, owing to Tryon's independence of spirit and his insistence that he be given a free hand to carry out his theories, he was engaged as Professor of Art and given full charge of the work in drawing and painting. This position he kept for thirty-eight years, until his resignation in 1923.

Early in his administration of the College affairs, President Seelye foresaw the need of a museum or gallery of pictures as an aid to the study of art. He had already begun to purchase paintings to add to the few already acquired by gift, so that when Tryon took his position a small beginning had been made toward the formation of the present extensive collection. President Seelye at once began to seek Tryon's advice in the yearly purchase of new works, for which Tryon was exceptionally well fitted. He not only possessed a wide knowledge of contemporary painting, and a catholic and refined taste, but he knew intimately most of the younger American painters, who, like himself, had recently completed their studies abroad and were already producing important works.

Tryon's acquaintance with Dewing and Thayer, for example, enabled him to purchase at what now seem absurdly low prices fine specimens of their work of the early eighties. 'A Lute-Player,' by Dewing, one of the first of Tryon's purchases for the gallery, is a distinguished precursor of Dewing's later qualities, with all the charm and more than the elegance of a fine Terburg. One of Thayer's 'Angels' is another fortunate early purchase. Works by Ryder, Inness, Wyant, Twachtman, Tarbell, Brush, Weir, Blakelock, Brandegee, Hassam, and Whistler have been purchased at intervals during the ensuing years. Along with these, a group of Tryon's own work was acquired consisting of certain pictures which he and President Seelye selected from time to time, representing the different periods and phases of his art. They begin with the large marine, 'The River Maas at Dordrecht,' painted in 1881, 30 × 48 in size. Of the dozen or more are: 'Moorlands at Dartmouth,' dated 1883, 30 × 52; 'A Salt Marsh — December,' painted in

90

TRYON IN 1890

1890, size 24 × 36; 'Twilight, May,' 30 × 42, dated 1894; 'Dawn,' a 20 × 30, painted in 1896; and a beautiful 'October Fields,' 20 × 30, painted in 1913–14, one of Tryon's many gifts to the College. There are also three of his pastels, about 8 × 12 in size, done in 1916, of the series of 'Sea Moods.' Since Tryon's death in 1925, the College has inherited Tryon's own collection of paintings by himself and others.

Tryon was twice armed in his qualifications for teaching. He had first a definite theory of art in its broadest sense, its history, its relation to life, and above all, its cultural aspects. Secondly, he was admirably fitted by his own education and his years of experience of painting to teach its technical processes. Theory and practice should go hand in hand, he contended, in the study of painting as in most other intellectual pursuits. Unfortunately, in most art schools it has been and still is the custom to teach the student technical methods and to neglect utterly the cultivation of his mind and imagination. I will quote here a letter of Tryon's written to me in 1884, when I had asked his advice about the advisability of taking up art as a profession, because it hints at his attitude toward teaching, summed up in the line, '... bring me whatever you have done from your own invention.' The rest of the letter also indicates his sensible weighing of practical considerations and facing of the problems involved without illusion:

'SOUTH DARTMOUTH, MASS.
Sept. 23, '84

'... Yours of the 19th received. I hardly know what to answer you in regard to giving up business and commencing seriously studying art as a profession, there are so many things to consider.

91

'The main thing must be whether you have so strong a love and desire for it that you are willing to sacrifice everything else for it; if it is so I should say do it by all means.

'As I remember your work I should say that you had more than average ability in that direction, but of course before you can do anything of value you will need several years of study. I shall be back in New York early in November, and if you will come and bring me some of your work, I can then judge better what to say to you and what to advise; in the mean while you need not be losing time, as you can be working by yourself when you have leisure from business. Bring me whatever work you have done from your own invention. If you have tried to paint any pictures from what you have seen in nature, bring them, as they will give me an idea of what your inclination is. If you have made any studies from nature or sketches, either in pencil or color, bring them also.

'I shall be very glad to see you and can, I think, give you some help in the matter. Let me know a few days before you are coming so I may not miss you.'

Tryon's class in drawing and painting in New York in 1885 consisted of eight or ten pupils. There were two or three adult men. The rest were women, young or middle-aged, most of whom had studied previously. Some, like myself, were also working at the Art Students' League under Brush, Cox, Dewing, Chase, and Twachtman. Two days each week were spent with Tryon. How fortunate we all were to come under the direct influence, the severe discipline of the tradition of Ingres, acquired by Tryon in the unique drawing school of Jacquesson de la Chevreuse, passed on to us and driven home with all the

92

force and clearness of Tryon's scientific mind and dynamic personality! Drawing, the probity of art! Proportions, the *big* proportions — and evermore and eternally, proportions! The character of the masses, the action — and values! We took it all for granted then. This was the right, the logical way to draw. We knew no other. To-day where do we find these basic qualities in contemporary painting, to say nothing of their application as an exact science in schools of art?

Yes, blessings brighten as they take their flight — and the rare quality of Tryon's teaching that made fine achievement seem so possible, though so difficult, many of his pupils have mourned as something never to be repeated or recovered. I have outlined briefly in a preceding chapter the system of drawing taught by Tryon, but no one who has not undergone the experience can fully understand the thoroughness with which he drilled his students, to the end that good drawing, at least, might become a part of their being — something that neither time nor habit could ever wholly obliterate.

Once in a while the severity of Tryon's standards drove a weak sister from his class. Anxious to get at painting and discouraged by months of slow and laborious progress, she would announce that she was going to study for a while under some other teacher. For a time we would hear good reports from her. Then in the fall when we started to work again she would appear in Tryon's studio to rejoin his class. She had found no substitute for his teaching and was ready to admit that there was no royal road to success, no salvation but by hard work and plodding.

With Tryon we usually drew from the cast during the first half of the winter. We then had a model from which, with intermittent studies of still life, we drew in charcoal or painted until spring. At intervals Tryon requested us to bring in studies made at home, out-of-door sketches, and especially attempts at picture-making. All of these he criticized individually, each member of the class profiting by his comments on the work of the others. Tryon observed closely the temperamental difference in his pupils and adapted his instruction to the peculiarities of each. Sometimes he would tell a student whose sense of form was weak to drop drawing for a while and model in wax or clay, that he might better grasp the third dimension. And we changed frequently, back and forth, from black and white to color, to avoid falling into a rut. If one had a stiff and labored manner of working, Tryon swept stump or brush freely into the study until it was loose and suggestive. To the careless and undisciplined whose construction and anatomy were flimsy, he emphasized the importance of precision, of sticking at elementary drawing. But unlike most teachers, from the very outset and along with the drill of drawing and painting, of learning the use of one's tools, he drew our attention to the æsthetic side of art study. He strove to develop the creative faculties, to stimulate the imagination, and always to cultivate that rare and precious possession, good taste.

To show the sharp contrast between the haphazard methods of certain celebrated teachers and Tryon's conscientious attention to every aspect of study, I have always remembered the remark made by one of our eminent painters, a man for whose work I have much respect. This artist used to say to his students when setting them to paint still life: 'Just throw the objects upon the table in any way. Do not attempt to arrange or compose them, for you are not now learning to produce pic-

94

STUDY OF INTERIOR OF TRYON'S STUDIO IN REMBRANDT BUILDING, NEW YORK, BY HENRY C. WHITE

tures, you are just learning to paint.' Tryon's procedure was the reverse of this. The subject to be painted might be a life model, the head of an old man, or a woman with a child in her arms. It might be a bowl of roses, a Japanese jar and fan, or the interior of the studio itself; but whatever the objects, Tryon invariably devoted much time and thought to arrangement in form and color, to lighting, and to the selection of an harmonious background, sometimes spending half the morning in this way. Working with us he would select, reject, arrange and rearrange, until we attained a pleasing result. The picture was there; all we had to do was to render it. For, as he said, 'A study well arranged is half painted.'

He continually called our attention to the important current exhibitions of pictures in New York. He suggested books to read and showed us reproductions of masterpieces of painting. When we were painting from the model, he sent us to the Museum to study the work of Rembrandt, Hals, Velasquez, and the great figure painters. George Frederick Watts held an important exhibition of his pictures at the Metropolitan Museum about this time, and Tryon, who admired the imaginative qualities in his work, suggested that I would do well to copy one of them. This I did, choosing the 'Endymion.'

Tryon also kept in close touch with the work of his contemporaries, who, like himself, had returned home and were beginning to exert what was to prove a lasting influence upon American art. He was severely critical and very discriminating in his appreciations, but no one was more enthusiastic than he over a masterpiece by Thayer, Dewing, Brush, John La Farge, or Saint-Gaudens, as they appeared. He especially admired La Farge's stained glass, and he advised us to seek it out, to saturate our perceptions with its glorious color. His instinct for beauty was infallible from the first, and time has amply justified his early enthusiasms and evaluations. This was the Yankee in Tryon that he always had an absolutely sure eye for value, the genuine as against the spurious, not only in financial matters, but also in art.

Tryon valued highly the words of criticism of William Morris Hunt to his classes, collected and published by his pupil, Helen M. Knowlton, and he was fond of quoting from them. To a spinster among Tryon's pupils who suffered from a slightly inflamed New England conscience, and who inquired, 'Mr. Tryon, do you think it is right to paint on Sunday?' he quoted Hunt's reply to a similar question, 'All work is a prayer.'

Seriousness and hard work pervaded Tryon's studio. There were no triflers and there was no loafing. After a silence of two hours broken only by his quiet word of criticism or the rests of the model, he would say: 'Lay down your palette, look about the room and rest your eye. If you work too continuously, you cannot see what you are doing. Detach yourself from your study for a few moments.'

He allowed no faults to pass uncorrected, but the general tone of his criticisms was optimistic and encouraging. He tuned us to concert pitch. There was a talented young woman in his painting class of whom Tryon was very proud. She painted animals in a more masterly way than many professionals. Her work stood well beside that of Troyon, Van Marcke, or Jacque. Her drawing was impeccable, her color rich and glowing, and her handling of pigment as skillful at eighteen as that of most painters at fifty. The textures in her still life suggested Chardin, and one felt that the hair of the hunting dogs she loved to paint, or the fur of her cats, needed but the stroke of one's hand to snap with electricity. She reveled, too, in rendering the elusive surface of a white fur rug, a thing without much substance or color, but to which she was able to give a wondrous charm and vitality.

Reserved and dignified in her manner, this young lady seldom spoke to any of the other students, by reason, I think, of shyness. Her wealthy and aristocratic family insisted, I remember, upon a chaperon, an elderly woman who always sat by with her sewing during the painting lesson. All in all, the girl's personality reflected such a cloistered existence, such a fragility, that one felt she should not be treated roughly. Even with her, however, Tryon was impartial in his criticism and at times ruthless. He knew neither hunger nor fatigue himself when he painted, and he expected his pupils to disregard these and all other distractions besides.

So it happened one day that the gifted young woman, painting, as she did, with intense application, showed fatigue bordering by noontime on exhaustion. She had nearly completed one of her most charming studies when she laid aside her palette and brushes and arose to go. 'Why are you stopping?' asked Tryon. 'It is lunch-time and I am tired,' she replied. 'Never mind your lunch or being tired,' said Tryon. 'Go on.' 'But,' she argued, 'I have a headache.' 'Never mind your headache either,' insisted Tryon. 'Your study only needs a little more work to complete it. It is one of your best things, and if you don't finish it now, you never will. Stick to it and put it through!' Thus fortified, the girl desperately threw herself at the canvas again, and the day was won. Though Tryon did not overpraise her in her presence, he held her to high standards.

97

He took great pleasure in the beauty of her painting, and often pulled out her studies when she was not in the studio to show to his class as examples of good work.[1]

Tryon claimed that landscape was a man's art, and that few women are good landscape painters. The reasons for this he thought to be occult and not generally understood. He also philosophized frequently upon the fact that women usually learn to draw with difficulty, though their feeling for color is often strong and true: this proving them, he thought, to be creatures of emotion rather than of logic. He also believed women to be, as a rule, more appreciative of art than men, though less able to produce distinguished work themselves. His theory of instruction in the woman's college was based, roughly, upon these assumptions. His aim was not, primarily, to train painters, but rather to develop their instinctive appreciation. He hoped that, through them, as wives and mothers, 'society might be humanized.' General culture was the end in view rather than technical achievement. Now and then, however, a talented woman, under Tryon's severe discipline, produced charming work of lasting worth. Mary R. Williams, his assistant for many years in the Art School at Smith College, painted extremely well. The College owns a group of her pictures, oils and pastels, and she is represented in other public collections in New England.

Tryon always said that Miss Beulah Strong, another of his assistants in the Art Department, was the best teacher of drawing that he had known, in a long experience. She, too, resigned, in 1923, after seventeen years of service.

Many of Tryon's pupils have paid tribute to him as a teacher,

[1] Miss Post.

98

My dear Miss Strong

I am glad the dish
arrived safely and I
trust will look well
in the Cabinet —

Awata is a province in
Japan and while I am not
sure this came from there
I have a faint recollection
that it did.

If the Suireno was
a gift it might be accep-
table but I do not think
it fine enough to be
considered as a purchase.

Very sincerely yours

D. W. Tryon

Nov 1 – 1916

LETTER TO MISS BEULAH STRONG

to the inspiration of his magnetic personality, his encouraging optimism and his conscientiousness. Virginia J. Smith, one of his pupils at Smith College in the class of 1907, writes the following note of appreciation: [1]

'To his old students it seems strange that the name of Dwight Tryon, benefactor of Smith, should be better known to the alumnæ as a whole through his generous bequest to the College than through his infinitely more generous giving of himself through many long years. Probably no member of the faculty was known to so few students, yet it is doubtful if any gave more freely of himself in his teaching or made a more lasting mark on those he taught than did Mr. Tryon on that little group who wended their way almost daily to the Hillyer Gallery and to whom Friday morning of every third week was indeed a red letter day.

'In the November "Quarterly," Mr. Churchill told something of Dwight Tryon the man; the world knows of Dwight Tryon the artist; but to comparatively few was given the opportunity to know Mr. Tryon the teacher, yet that relationship was one of the great privileges which Smith College of the earlier days had to offer. A short man, with the keen, far-sighted eyes of the seafarer, lighted with the whimsical twinkle of the great of heart; a man inspired with an intense enthusiasm. If there is anything in the etymology of the word, Mr. Tryon was a great educator. He never poured his greater knowledge or his technical methods into a pupil — perhaps the immediate results of our efforts would have been more creditable to the Department had he done so; but rather with utmost patience and a sympathetic understanding by helping us to

[1] *Smith Alumnæ Quarterly*, July, 1926.

find our own method of expression, encouraging us, commenting on every enlargement of vision, holding us to standards of sincerity and truth, helping us over stumbling blocks, he so imbued us with his own great enthusiasm that we were a-tiptoe with effort and desire for better things. His enthusiasm was contagious — we worked with almost a frenzy of effort to put into practice the hints he had given us in his last criticism. We forgot the "minimum of six hours" of the catalogue and stopped only when darkness settled down and Fritz drove us out in order to lock the Gallery.

'It cannot be mere coincidence that a rather poor memory can recall almost word for word many of his criticisms delivered twenty years ago and that those criticisms were so replete with meaning that their reiteration to-day is almost as stimulating as their original pronouncement. He seemed to feel instinctively the moment for praise and the moment for blame. He came once in three weeks and criticized the work of most of the students in the Department, yet no criticism was ever hurried; he responded to every inquiry and desire for help, and the work of each student was so distinct in his mind that he could compare present studies with those done a month previously.

'He used often to say, "There is no one way to paint; if there had been it would have been patented long ago. Each must find for himself his own expression." I remember one day when showing him in utmost discouragement a study which chiefly resembled a mud pie, I said, "Mr. Tryon, I am ashamed to show you this — I can criticize it myself." "I am glad to hear you say that," was his reply. "Criticism is a vital part of painting. To paint a picture you have to be both a painter and a critic. Daubigny, the elder, lacked a critical faculty, and it is a

100

thing which has militated against his reputation more than anything else. He did not know which were his best canvases and so did not destroy the poorer ones, and that is why you see so many poor Daubignys to-day. No one can do good work all the time."

'And then he went on to speak of color in neutrals. "The test of any painting is its neutrals. It is easy to paint brilliant color, but it is far more difficult to make your neutrals full of color. Look at these Japanese prints (part of his remarkable collection of masterpieces which he had loaned the Gallery); see the wonderful quality of the blacks and whites in them, vibrating with color. Often in painting a bit of sky I will put blue on it and scrape it off; I will put pink on it and scrape it off; I will put yellow on it and scrape it off; I will put green on it and scrape it off, and my sky will look almost white — but it isn't, for it will have in it the vibrations of all those colors." One day I asked him why he continued his trips to Smith when we were showing such poor results for his efforts. "I am interested in what you are doing," he replied, "and I also find that it is an excellent thing for my own work. It forces me to get away from my work and I always come back to it with a new vision."

'How well I remember the last criticism he gave me — applicable to other lines of endeavor it would seem. "Go on with your art studies by all means if you can possibly do so, but if things shape themselves so that it is impossible, do not be discouraged. If you have it in you to paint a great picture, nothing in the world can keep you from painting. If you find you haven't that irresistible urge for expression, the world will lose nothing by not having you paint."'

Tryon thoroughly enjoyed teaching. It never was drudgery

or routine to him. He liked all its associations and often remarked that it helped him in his own painting. Like William
Morris Hunt, with whom I often find myself comparing Tryon,
he used to say to his pupils, 'I come here to the class and see
you making the same mistakes that I do myself and I go back
and correct my own work through yours.' He rarely painted
upon the study of a pupil. His criticisms were clearly expressed
and invariably to the point. Beyond that he left one free to
follow one's impulses and he never tried to impress his methods
upon his students. He strove to reveal underlying truths
and principles to them. They must make their own applica-
tions.

'The delight of art,' Tryon was wont to say, 'is that you are
free to do anything you most whimsically please. Only,' he
added, 'you must not violate the fundamental truths of nature
or the principles of æsthetics.' I have often wondered how
much of modernistic painting would stand this test.

While Tryon never taught his pupils a particular method of
painting, his own least of all, he encouraged them to experiment widely, in fact, insisted upon it. 'Anything to avoid falling into a rut or manner,' he used to say. And I never knew a
painter who had so many technical resources as he. 'Paint the
head in thickly, with strong and loaded color to-day,' he would
suggest, 'then to-morrow, when it is half dry, scrape it and
paint into it.' Or, 'Prepare your ground with crude, even
violent color. Put it away and let it dry hard. Then, painting
over it with delicate veils and tones, work for subtlety and refinement. If your color is crude and raw, paint into it with
black and white or with mud. If it is dull and gray, brighten it
with brilliant positive color, freely worked in.' And there was

THE TRYON ROOM, TRYON GALLERY, SMITH COLLEGE MUSEUM OF ART

INTERIOR, TRYON GALLERY, NORTHAMPTON, MASS.

no method of under- or over-painting, glazing and scumbling that, sooner or later, he would not suggest. In fact, his bag of tricks was inexhaustible. But as a rule he advised beginners to stick to direct methods. Involutions, logically, came later.

Sometimes, as often happened, when a student, absorbed in the manipulation of paint, lost his drawing, Tryon would then quote to his class the homely aphorism of a French instructor, whose name I forget, 'Get a good drawing, a good drawing! Then, defile it if you must!' — 'Work for drawing, then turn about and work for color,' was Tryon's frequent reminder. And his constant admonition was, 'Strengthen yourself on your weak side!' — 'Why don't you fix the nose in your study? It's all out of drawing.' 'But, Mr. Tryon, I've been leaving it, for I dreaded to touch it!' 'Then do it *the first thing!* The moment you become afraid of your work you are lost.' And immediately the lady was in for an exhaustive study of noses, in charcoal or paint, until she was made free of their obsession. 'I got so mad at my study I spoiled it!' 'Good! If you get mad enough, you probably will make a success of it! Stand your study on its head! Look at it in the mirror! Go away and leave it! Put it by and forget it! When you come to it with a fresh eye, very likely you will see just what it needs.'

Mr. Churchill, Tryon's colleague at Smith, gives us interesting glimpses of him as a teacher. In the 'Smith Alumnæ Quarterly' he says:

'Tryon in his turn, wanted to know all about the Department (of art); what the students were doing and thinking about; and who the new members of the Department were and what they were doing; about the equipment we had and what we needed. He was interested along the broad lines rather

103

than in administrative detail, which he disliked, though he could master it if necessary. He never attended departmental meetings.... In a letter written from New York soon after his resignation took effect, he says:

'"*My dear Churchill:*... It seems good to get a line from you. It is like a breath of life which has meant much to me in years past. While I have been congratulating myself that I have not been obliged to make the railway trip to Northampton this winter, I still feel the loss of the delightful associations connected with the visits. I have, however, been so deeply immersed in the work in my studio that time passes and I have little time for regrets."

'The next letter dated a few months afterwards, was written when Tryon's activity as a teacher had definitely ceased. His classes were now in the hands of a younger man whose ideas and methods differed widely from his own. He had lost not only the long-accustomed contact with young minds, and the inspiration of young faces turned eagerly to his, but he knew that his day was over and that the ways that had seemed good to him were now being remade. In these circumstances it was my privilege to reassure him, rendering the change as little painful as might be. He always responded with great liberality and sweetness, concealing in his heart the misgivings he must sometimes have had.

'October 31, 1922 (from South Dartmouth). "... I am greatly interested to hear how things are progressing at Smith. The great thing is to feel that there is real interest in art *as a humanizer*. Few persons are fitted by nature to be producers of so-called fine art, but all should be made richer by the sense of appreciation. Every one should be an artist and when this day

104

comes, there will be better work done by all and more happiness in the world."

'From a letter written shortly after giving his last criticisms: May 16, 1923 (from South Dartmouth). "... I meant before leaving to have impressed on the minds of the students that although I am no longer visiting them in classes I, by no means, lose my interest in them individually and I want them to feel free to call on me in New York for any help or advice they need."

'In these lines, Tryon's students will recognize his old kindliness and thoughtfulness for their interest. In a postscript, with a touch of quaint humor which was habitual with him, he has added (apropos of nothing whatever and just because he felt like it) a bit of doggerel from an old studio song:

'"La peinture à l'huile
Est bien difficile,
Mais, c'est beaucoup plus beau
Que la peinture à l'eau."'

Mr. Churchill also writes of Tryon as a teacher and his ideals as an educator, in his article, 'Dwight W. Tryon, Professor of Art,' [1] from which I will select one or two paragraphs:

'... Among his pupils he was revealed as a teacher of clear and intense conviction, who always gave them the best that he had in the way of criticism, advice, and encouragement. But his interests were by no means limited to his students. The Museum claimed a generous share of his attention. He never entered it without taking a good look about, studying things with ever-renewed enthusiasm and attention, making pregnant remarks about the relation of art and nature, and the qualities that belong in common to all art that is worthy of the name.

[1] *Bulletin* of Smith College, March 30, 1924.

'He loved to give to the Museum things that would have value in cultivating taste. Indeed, he seldom arrived here, in these later years, without something up his sleeve — in his valise or greatcoat pocket, to speak precisely. It would prove perhaps to be a rare book, a bit of Oriental pottery, or a diminutive bronze. Sometimes he announced a gift of major importance. Once it was an oil painting by Wyant; again it was his own collection of Japanese prints (made years before when prints could be had without spending a fortune); at another time it was his painting "October Fields," because, as he said, he wished the College to have an example of his later work.

'Tryon shared in all the activities of the Department. He was interested in the new teachers, the new courses, the plans of the future. He was ever to be depended on for wise counsel and moral support. Fortunately, we still have access to these; for he is still with us in spirit.'

Tryon, as Mr. Churchill says, was proverbially generous to others, and gave constantly of his means or his time to any person whose needs appealed to him or to causes which interested him. Both to his friends and to the institution to which he finally left his fortune, he continually presented beautiful things from his own choice collection of art treasures and rare books.

Tryon worked under Presidents Seelye, Burton, and Neilson, all of whom gave him a free hand to carry out his theories and did all they could to help him. If he wanted a new studio, they built it. If he recommended a change of method in instruction, they acceded to it. This attitude on the part of the College was, of course, a great aid in his teaching. He was unhampered. Therefore he always worked with enthusiasm.

106

EXTERIOR, TRYON GALLERY, NORTHAMPTON, MASS.

In May, 1923, Tryon resigned his position as head of the Art Department, and in June of the same year Smith College conferred upon him the degree of Master of Arts. I quote the following letter from President Seelye written at the time of Tryon's resignation:

'22 ROUND HILL
NORTHAMPTON, *June* 4, 1923

'*My dear Mr. Tryon:*

'When you were in Northampton on May 25th I was away from home for two days and I was very sorry to learn, on my return, that you had resigned the position as head of the Art Department of Smith College which you had filled most satisfactorily for many years. If your resignation was due to the same recognition of a natural law which led me to take a similar step, I cannot remonstrate; at the same time, your action brings a sense of personal and corporate loss. It will lessen the opportunities of renewing an acquaintance which I have highly prized and it will take from the College one of its most honored and successful teachers. Your work here has been of inestimable value, both on account of your superior ability as an instructor and the inspiration and refining influence of your paintings in the Hillyer Art Galleries.

'I rejoice to know that you have generously made plans whereby that inspiration may continue and become even more effective in the future than it has been in the past.

'I cannot adequately express, Mr. Tryon, my own indebtedness to you for the encouragement and sympathy you have given me in my efforts to make the study of art an integral and honored part of the higher education of women.

'Without your aid I do not believe it could have won the

place it now holds in public esteem. I cannot think of you as an old man and I hope you may still add to the number of masterpieces which have given you an incontestable place among the foremost American artists.

'With high esteem, I remain
'Cordially yours
'(Signed)   L. CLARK SEELYE'

Tryon had in mind to present an art gallery to Smith College for a number of years before 1914. His plans were interrupted by the war, but by 1923 they began to take form, and he was in consultation with the architect, Mr. Frederick Ackerman, who was his friend, with President Neilson and with Mr. Churchill, for months preceding his last illness. Ground was broken in June, 1925. As Tryon died in July of that year, he was denied the pleasure of seeing his dream become a reality. The building was completed and occupied the following September.

'The gallery has two floors: a ground floor partially below grade, and a main floor entered from the street level by a welcoming flight of outside steps. One enters through a simple vaulted vestibule a large rectangular hall, marble paved, from which the galleries open, and from a broad flight of curved stairs sweeps down to the floor below. Directly opposite the entrance is the chief room, the *salon carré* of the museum, large enough for dignity, but small enough to give that intimate touch so characteristic of the whole. To the right, at the end of the hall, is the Special Exhibition Room, a smaller gallery for temporary and changing loan exhibitions, and at the other end, to the left, the Tryon Room — the room dedicated to the donor of the building, and designed to contain his own paintings and a selection from his gifts, so that his memory may be worthily and sympathetically perpetuated. On the lower floor are three more galleries, a large one and two smaller, similar in shape to those on the main floor, but lighted from windows instead of from above; and in addition a large storeroom. There are, of course, aside from the galleries, the necessary coatrooms and lavatories....' [1]

In the vestibule a marble tablet tells the visitor who gave the building and what its purpose was:

THAT THE STUDENTS OF THIS COLLEGE

MAY KNOW IN THEIR YOUTH

THE SOLACE AND INSPIRATION OF ART

DWIGHT WILLIAM TRYON AND ALICE BELDEN TRYON

HAVE DEDICATED TO THEM THIS BUILDING

MCMXXV

[1] Talbot Faulkner Hamlin, *Bulletin* of Smith College Museum, June, 1926.

X

THE MAN

THE reader may be wondering, by this time, what Tryon looked like. There are few good pictures of him. It was somewhat difficult to draw his likeness, for he did not pose well at any time, for portrait painter, photographer, or reporter. I think perhaps a word-picture will give us a true impression. There was something particularly dynamic, as well as elusive, about the short, sinewy figure whose motions were so quick. Mrs. Dewing once said it was difficult for her to imagine Tryon as the painter of poetry, of dream-like visions. His figure was so robust and sturdy, his cheeks so ruddy, and his whole presence so charged with vitality that, as she expressed it, 'he seemed explosive!'

I shall always remember how he looked as he landed at his wharf at about five o'clock on a summer afternoon, upon his return from fishing. As usual, I found him throwing flounders ashore from the big fish box which he had dragged across the landing-stage. The black cat, roused from its rocking-chair slumbers, sat sedately upon the string-piece and viewed the

TRYON IN 1923

proceedings with interest. A freckle-faced boy waited with a basket, for Tryon's neighbors had a standing invitation to call at his wharf for fresh fish upon his return each evening. The rule was first come, first served, and you dressed your own fish. When his daily catch was so large that it depressed the local market, he gave his surplus to the fish dealer and stabilized trade.

'Well! Well! Glad to see you!' The voice was deep and resonant. You felt always its dignity as well as its cordiality. 'Was it hot inland? It was cool enough where I was. I had two reefs in all day. Just shook 'em out on the way home. Quite rugged outside —— Yes, pretty fair luck! They bit well for a while, on the ebb. Thirty or forty I should say. Some will go three pounds —— Where the devil is that Portuguese? He said he would be here to-night to take these fish. I'm not going to peddle 'em all over town! If I catch 'em, they can at least come and get 'em! I suppose they will expect me to deliver 'em all dressed, next! — Yes, I got your letter last night. How is everybody? ——'

Tryon climbed upon the dock, hastily wiped a fishy hand and gave you a hearty grip. His smile was engaging, but he flashed a penetrating glance at you if you were a stranger. You might have felt in it a hint of friendly challenge. He was a trifle shy and did not accept you unreservedly. He had to be shown. Without ceremony, very simple and direct, he radiated a genial heartiness. When he played at his sailing and fishing, he was buoyant and high-spirited to the point of gayety. As he hauled his rowboat upon the float stage and gathered up his fishing-tackle, his motions were quick, almost jerky. He wasted no time, but neither was he hurried. As he disembarked, one saw,

111

at close range, that his duck trousers did not belong to a member of the rocking-chair fleet. Blood and fish scales had well bespattered them and likewise the canvas sneakers. His blue cotton shirt was faded on the shoulders and the loosely knotted necktie drooped in despondent festoons. Sun, spray, and sea winds had sported with him, caressed him, and left their seal.

The fish disposed of, a little procession marched up the wharf to the house. The cat led with tail erect. In one hand Tryon carried two or three fat mackerel or flounders to dress for supper, in the other his fishing-rod. He reeled off his line to dry, stretching it from the boathouse door to a wild-cherry tree. Then, dressing the fish, he threw choice morsels to the expectant cat. Wet with salt water, sunburned, physically tired and ravenously hungry, Tryon had completed his summer day.

Year in and year out, with few interruptions, this was his daily routine in fair weather, from May to October, from daybreak to evening. A day spent on shore was the exception. Rain or storm merely gave excuse to make a new fishing-rod or to repair old ones, to fashion a new gaff for his catboat, to tinker in his shop.

In Tryon you faced a figure that has often surprised those who knew him only through his work. The personality of this painter of poetic landscapes might have disconcerted you. Instead of the slender, delicately formed man one might have inferred, he was short, rather thick-set and muscular, weighing about one hundred and forty pounds. At first glance he looked like the bronzed and sturdy sailor and fisherman that, for half the year, he was. His head and features, however, arrested attention. They indicated intellect and genius beyond a doubt. The high forehead bulged prominently above the eyes, where.

112

phrenologically, the senses of perception are supposed to lie, and it was seamed with crow's-feet wrinkles of concentrated thought. His severely aquiline and sharply modeled nose gave the dominant note of a strong character. His blue eyes, which shaded to brown or gray, were roving and restless when scanning the waters of Buzzard's Bay for signs of fish, and again, in the quiet of his home, contemplative, almost dreamy, when the talk ran on art or philosophy.

His hair, dark brown and brushed straightly back, was thick, and still, at his seventieth year, almost untouched with gray. He wore a short bristly mustache. His cheeks were ruddy, and below his forehead, which was white by contrast, his face, neck, and throat were darker hued than an Indian, a deep brown of exposure to the weather that never faded until his last illness. His hands, wide, with short thick fingers, blunt at the ends, calloused and gnarled as those of any sailor or farmer, gave no evidence whatever of his mastery of minute and delicate craftsmanship. He could tie a fly to counterfeit the gnats and midges of the Maine woods (as he did at the Belgrade Lakes, for black bass), to the despair of other fishermen, surpassing the best professionals. His iridescent dragon-fly, tied with colored silks and peacock or wood duck feathers, was a work of consummate art, more dainty and dazzling than the insect itself.

Tryon loved flowers — but mostly the wild ones. He left it to others to cultivate those that adorned his dooryard. I have sometimes read with amusement articles in the press or in magazines referring to Tryon's 'farm' at South Dartmouth, where in summer he 'hoed in his garden.' I regret to dispel such a pleasing legend of devotion to bucolic life, but as this is one of those prosaic old-fashioned biographies, dealing solely with facts, I am obliged to state, reluctantly, that Tryon was no devotee of the hoe and that he always hired a village youth to cut the few square feet of grass that surrounded his cottage. Perhaps the shock will now be less if I call your attention to his vegetable patch. It lay next to the boathouse, on the south side. It was about two feet wide by four feet long, and with difficulty sustained a half-dozen heads of anæmic lettuce, and a few spindling sprouts of what started to be onions. The luxuriant grass and weeds nearly concealed the tiny plot. Yes, it was quite evident that our ploughman of the brine could well say with Emerson, 'He who sees my garden knows I must have some other garden.' As Tryon said himself, it probably was his inheritance from generations of tillers of the soil that compelled him to plant this spare strip of earth each spring, for no one laughed more heartily than he at its inconsequential harvest.

Tryon had nothing of the conventional artist about him. He affected no properties or stage-settings of his profession, enveloped himself in no artistic or Bohemian atmosphere. On the contrary, he appeared and acted quite differently from the painter as popularly conceived. Of his New York apartment, richly furnished and decorated with exquisite taste, he somehow never seemed a part. He was like a sailor on shore leave, making a brief call amongst alien surroundings, with an itching to return to sea. What spats and eyeglasses with Oxford ribbons and modish garments are to the artist or *littérateur* of the avenues and clubs, Cape Ann oilskins, sou'westers, and hip rubber boots were to Tryon. These he selected with the care of a connoisseur, always had a full supply of the best of them, and never counted the cost.

Early acquaintances say that in his young manhood he took

greater heed of his dress and for a short time was something of a dandy. But if this was mentioned in his presence, he looked uncomfortable and changed the subject. He begrudged any time given to his raiment. When his friend Bell said he had paid forty or fifty dollars for his new suit, Tryon reproached him for his extravagance. 'I myself,' he said, 'can always buy a good ready-made suit for fifteen or twenty dollars. It seems to me foolish to pay more.'

Tryon's clothes had a phenomenal longevity. They made their *début* in his New York apartment and served for his professorial trips to Smith College. When the trousers began to feel the decay of time, they were relegated to South Dartmouth and did yeoman service in the fishing industry, while the repaired coats made their final appearance (after a considerable period) in the cabin of his catboat. Joseph's coat of many colors would have blushed before one of these amazing fabrics. I remember one I saw on board the Skat about 1924. It was a composite of coats and suits dating back twenty years, and consisted of patches about six inches square sewed together loosely with both black and white thread, by Tryon himself. I could trace the history of his wardrobe during the decades by the reminiscent fragments of tweeds, serges, worsteds, and even khaki and cotton. While I do not believe that he consciously composed its multifarious hues and textures, they blended harmoniously like a Persian carpet.

Tryon abhorred the fashionable. On a certain occasion when I proposed taking him to a quiet hotel at the seashore, he immediately inquired, 'Can I wear my rubber boots to the table?' This was his criterion of public houses, and he had an uncanny instinct for finding places where he could do as he pleased. He

115

liked their informality and the interesting types of people he met in them. After a day's fishing at Ogunquit, in autumn, Tryon would join the little group in the boarding-house parlor, where, before the wood fire in the box stove, he would discuss with them art or literature, religion or politics. He could swap stories with any one from a savant to a traveling shoe salesman, to the delight of all. And in the memories of all I am sure he left an ineffaceable impression. He was equally at home with people of culture or with the hewers of wood and drawers of water. His social club, from spring until fall, was the country store, where he almost invariably spent an hour after supper, foregathered round the stove with a fraternity who smoked pipes and swung feet from counter or cracker barrel. The place of honor was reserved for Tryon, a rickety armchair, in which he tipped back at a comfortable angle, exchanged yarns and accounts of the day's fishing with the local gossips, and with them forecast the weather and prospects for the morrow. One evening I arrived in South Dartmouth unexpected by him. Not finding him at home, I went to the store. There, in a group of fishermen, farmers, and loungers, sat Tryon, with his back to the door. I entered quietly and raised my hand in warning to the assembled company. Most of them knew me and winked in return. Stealing to the back of Tryon's chair, I gently placed my hands over his eyes. Without a motion, in the most casual tone in the world, he said, 'Cool hands, warm heart!' It was difficult to surprise him or catch him off his guard, and he had a ready response for all situations.

While Tryon was on the best of terms with his country neighbors, I think the reader will infer from my account that he was not much in evidence at lawn parties and afternoon teas.

I greatly enjoyed witnessing futile attempts to round him up and corral him for the discharge of social duty. A lady, a new-comer in South Dartmouth, moved into the house across the lane from Tryon's cottage. For several weeks he was urged to put on some respectable clothing and make a formal call on the new neighbor, but without result. Then one morning he was seen chatting sociably with her across the picket fence. A wheelbarrow stood beside him with a boat's mainsail piled upon it; and from the torn seat of his khaki trousers protruded a generous strip of blue denim shirt-tail. He was enthusiastic when he returned home. 'She's a fine woman,' he said, 'and we had a jolly visit.'

In his forty years of teaching in a woman's college, and in his private classes, Tryon surely had ample opportunity to observe and study feminine character. He often spoke with insight and appreciation of it, and I know how highly he valued these as-sociations. But, as I have stated before, he was not a man of drawing-rooms and salons; the gathering-places of conven-tional society knew him not. Both men and women who wished to meet him had to take him on the wing. He could be very shy, and he had a disconcerting way sometimes of suddenly vanish-ing into thin air, at the first tap upon the door knocker.

As I have said, Tryon's range of human contacts was wide. It included artists, actors, doctors, lawyers, ministers, business men, connoisseurs, musical and literary people, men of culti-vated minds, all the way to humanity in the rough. He used to fish and exchange stories with Grover Cleveland and Joe Jeffer-son, at the head of Buzzard's Bay; Victor Harris, the composer, was his friend and patron; Dr. Leroy M. Yale, physician and etcher, followed the trout brooks with him; he discussed poetry

117

with E. K. Rossiter, the architect, and science with Professor Bickmore, of the Museum of Natural History — to mention a small group.

I must, however, make this distinction. While Tryon's circle of acquaintances was extensive, he had few intimate friends. He insisted upon meeting people on his own terms, and he did not give himself unreservedly to every one. He guarded his privacy, both when he worked and when he played, with a keen and watchful eye. Time was precious to him and he wasted little of it, so little, in fact, that he seldom yielded to complete relaxation. In his waking hours there was, in colloquial phrase, something doing all the time. Once when we were cruising together in his boat, he said to me: 'You seem to get a good deal of comfort out of your after-dinner pipe. I think I would like to try it. Will you rig me up with the proper outfit?' So I purchased a new pipe which I seasoned for him, and mixed him a mild blend of tobacco. For about a week he lighted up after meals and tried assiduously to convince himself that he was enjoying it. Then I noticed that the pipe lay untouched on a shelf in the cabin. 'You are not progressing very fast in your novitiate of vice,' said I. 'Doesn't the habit grow upon you?' 'No,' he answered, 'I don't get much satisfaction out of sucking that pipe. Maybe I would if I kept on, *but I don't have the time for it!*'

Mr. Churchill, writing of Tryon's days in Northampton, says: 'He arrived always on the same train, late Thursday afternoon, and put up at the Draper. During the evening he would read at the Forbes Library or chat with a group of old friends who held a kind of informal club around the old-fashioned coal stove in Clark and Parson's drug-store. At nine

118

on Friday morning he was at the studio. By twelve-fifteen he had managed to give a criticism, or at least a word of remonstrance, encouragement, or advice to every student of drawing or of painting. As there were sixty or seventy in his classes, the time was full.' [1]

Tryon appreciated good wine and often had it on his table, though he drank sparingly of it himself. And he was a small eater. He was dignified in conversation and seldom swore, though he could do so picturesquely enough when occasion required, as it so often does in painting and fishing. He had a keen sense of humor, as I think his letters indicate; and I never knew a person who had such a phenomenal memory for stories and anecdotes. But he was by nature serious, and observed a very just sense of proportion in his joking, which never got out of hand. Of a frivolous nature myself, I never could interest him long in frivolity for its own sake. When I wrote him a letter with a lot of nonsense in it, he replied, 'Your consignment of persiflage is received,' and then devoted the remainder of his letter to serious affairs. But, even so, few of his letters were without a light touch of humor. He was always cheerful and optimistic.

I have said that Tryon's food, clothing, and shelter exemplified his simple tastes. While this holds true of his home in the country, I must qualify it so far as it applies to his life in New York. He loved artistic surroundings, and in winter he spent most of his time at home. So that, from the first modestly furnished rooms in the Rembrandt Building, where he and his wife began to keep house upon their return from Europe, to the beautiful home in the Harperly Hall Apartments at Central

[1] *Smith Alumnæ Quarterly*, November, 1925.

119

Park West and Sixty-Fourth Street, the third and last of his city residences, he took great interest and pleasure in the decorations and furnishing of his winter abodes. The color of the walls of the living-room was warm and neutral, a perfect setting for pictures. Over the mantel was a decorative panel by Dewing, the elegant figures of women against a pale greenish background, its opalescent colors echoed in pieces of iridescent Phœnician glass on the shelf below. A large decoration of Tryon's own, a spring subject, hung upon the principal wall space, and there was a figure picture by Bell, a girl in a yellow gown; and two or three of Tryon's early landscapes. His collection of books, many of them rare editions in fine bindings, took up one end of the room. And choice pieces of Oriental pottery and porcelain, some of them given to Tryon by Freer, were effectively arranged with discriminating taste.

On the walls of the dining-room hung Tryon's two fine Canalettos, and a very handsome early Italian picture, a Madonna, the artist unknown, but with the rich reds and blues of a Bellini, to whose period it evidently belonged. Tryon greatly admired the work of Blakelock, and one of his last acquisitions was an 'Indian Encampment' by this artist. There was also an interesting Wyant, and one or two more of Tryon's own early pictures.

Tryon received callers on Sunday afternoons. He disliked ceremony and often answered one's ring himself. He greeted you with a hearty 'Come aboard!' and led you to the living-room, where chairs were drawn up before the large east window, with its wide outlook over Central Park. He generally wore a lounging jacket, vest and trousers that did not synchronize, and a pair of bedroom slippers.

TRYON IN HIS STUDIO AT HARPERLEY HALL, ABOUT 1920

The studio adjoined the living-room, from which it was shut off by sliding doors in his working hours. A fine old Flemish tapestry hung upon the principal wall. It had always been the background against which he painted his pictures in every studio he occupied, for, as he said, 'it harmonized with everything.' The walls of the room were covered with Japanese grass cloth. There was no litter or confusion of painting materials or unfinished pictures, and, except for a few chairs, the furniture was severely restricted to a couple of easels, upon one of which was, perhaps, a completed picture, upon the other a frame with a panel upon which he was working, and which was covered with a piece of drapery. There was seldom more than one picture on view at a time and often none.

In this richly toned quiet setting, devoid of a single extraneous object to distract the eye, Tryon's pictures glowed and melted, the one concentrated dominant note of beauty in the harmonious whole. They were shown to the best advantage. And you sat under a little canopy or velarium as you viewed them, your eyes completely shaded from the skylight. On a small stand was Tryon's rather untidy palette, a Japanese vase containing a few well-worn brushes, a bottle of Mussini medium, and a tube or two of color.

So much for his winter environment. He was a fixed part of it, and remained as continuously at home and at work all winter as, at play, he kept habitually away from his house in the country in the summer.

Tryon often said that Art is a jealous mistress, that one must give himself whole-heartedly and utterly to her. All else must give way. So he allowed nothing to interfere with his routine of daily labor. In his younger days he painted both morning

121

and afternoon. During the last ten or twelve years of his life he usually worked from nine until one. Then after lunch he went over to the nearest branch of the public library in West Sixty-Ninth Street and exchanged his books, for he often read two or three in an evening. And he was fond of rummaging in second-hand bookstores, where he sometimes unearthed a rare first edition, obsolete works on art, travel, yachting and fishing, and old prints and engravings. He also kept himself informed of what interesting pictures were to be seen and dropped in frequently at the galleries. In the evening he read or was read to, or, as a relaxation from his painting, took up his 'knitting work' as he called it, rod-making or tying flies. He was always shopping in the tackle stores to renew his equipment for the next season's campaign.

We have seen that early in his youth Tryon became interested in literature. He read omnivorously throughout his life, not only the classics, but books on many and varied subjects. He was fond of Shakespeare, and Falstaff was his favorite character. He was familiar with French literature, English fiction and poetry, and often quoted Browning. The Concord writers influenced him strongly, and I think perhaps his ideals of life and his religious views would be well contained in the philosophy of Emerson. And I might almost say that Thoreau's 'Walden' was Tryon's Bible.

He was, however, especially fond of books of travel and adventure, as a diversion of his mind from the fatigue of painting. Speaking of literature and reading he said, 'You can't live on the heights of Olympus all the time.' He was always recommending to me some new or old tale of adventure, in romance or real life, which I had not read. At one time it was Defoe's

'Adventures of Captain Singleton,' at another a forgotten volume of Arctic exploration, or, again, the delightful 'Golden Days' of the English artist Romilly Fedden, a book on fishing in Brittany. Never but once that I remember was I able to surprise him with such a book with which he was not familiar. I sent him Lord Dufferin's 'Letters from High Latitudes,' the account of a yachting cruise in the Arctic, and immediately received an enthusiastic response, stating that he had never read it. There was little in the nooks, corners, and bypaths of literature that escaped him, and he frequently made a brief comment in his letters on a book he was reading, apropos of nothing in particular, as,'... Have you read Hector Berlioz's life? I am just reading it. A typical musical artist's life. I think they are several degrees worse than the painters.'

Tryon was very fond of music though he made no claim to a sophisticated taste in it. He had a good voice and was always singing snatches of operas, or catchy airs of popular music when he was aboard his boat and in his hours of recreation. At one time he played the guitar.

The nature of the man was complex, though it seemed simple. He was a mixture of opposed and strongly contrasted qualities. With his head in the clouds and his feet planted so firmly on the solid earth, he presented strange contradictions. An artist in every fiber of his being, one of the most imaginative landscape painters of his time, he was nevertheless a shrewd and successful business man. He was intensely practical, he had much administrative and executive ability; and he was also a skillful artisan in the more delicate processes of carpentry, cabinet-making, and boat-building.

The soul of honor and integrity, he could drive as sharp

a bargain as the most astute money-changer in the market-place. He used to say, laughing at himself, 'If you pit a Jew against a New England Yankee in a trade, the Jew will go to the wall every time.' Mr. Dewing once said to me, 'Tryon thought he was a Simon-pure old Yank, but, my God! I'm more of an old Yank than he ever thought of being!' Far be it from me to assume the rôle of Paris in so delicate a situation. As a native of Connecticut myself, I feel qualified to confirm their respective claims, but I prefer to remain strictly neutral as to the order of precedence.

Tryon was so successful in selling his pictures and so wise in making investments that he left a large fortune. Notwithstanding this, he was singularly indifferent to his material prosperity. His greatest striving was for the things of the spirit, his deepest interest was in culture, in æsthetic enjoyments. At a time when he had a large yearly income, he said to me: 'I have little use for money. Beyond my household expenses, my fishing-tackle, and my boat, none of which change very much, I cannot begin to spend the money I earn.'

When Tryon and I were fishing on the Ogunquit River one cool October morning, as we paddled our canoe along the shore, we came upon a tramp, who had built a fire on the beach and was roasting a fish for his breakfast. Some matted boughs under a great boulder near by indicated where he had slept the preceding night. Tryon's eyes lighted up at the sight of the curling smoke of the fire and the unkempt ragged figure that hovered over it in the crisp air and bright sunshine. 'That,' said he, 'is my ideal of a happy life. What greater satisfaction can the world offer than that outcast's freedom to enjoy this glorious autumn day out of doors? Probably we idealize him and he is unconscious of his good fortune, but, to me, he presents an inspiring spectacle.'

Notwithstanding Tryon's thrift and frugality he was very generous. I have known him to build a home for a young married couple in whose welfare he was interested and set them up in housekeeping; and he often bought the works of obscure and struggling artists, as well as giving them much helpful criticism and advice.

Once as I entered the living-room at South Dartmouth a charming little water-color stood upon the table. The style was unfamiliar to me, also the signature. When I spoke admiringly of it, Tryon said: 'That is the work of a potential genius, a musician in New Bedford. He paints in his spare time and brings his work to me for criticism and advice, and I sometimes buy his things. I enjoy them and I like to help him.' I spoke appreciatively of the water-color several times, and he finally said, 'You seem to like it so much you can have it and I will get another.'

At one time Tryon received the following letter from a clergyman: [1] Several times, it has been my good fortune to see one of your paintings; it is owned by the Art Gallery of Albany, New York. Of all the pictures there, it has left a singularly haunting influence upon me. I am a clergyman in a rural community, with a salary of a thousand dollars a year, seldom getting out, therefore I feel the need of something to inspire and buoy up one who is thrown constantly upon the commonplace, with the provincial views of those whose lives are on a comparatively low plane, and who see no need of the æsthetic in life. By careful economy, I have saved some two hundred and fifty dollars

[1] Reverend J. A. Donald.

125

over and above my insurance, and if you have a canvas which you would exchange for that amount, I should be rejoiced to make the exchange, for I am sure it will fill a definite need in my own life and have its quiet influence in the life of my son. I have not the faintest idea what prices your pictures command, but the value of any picture can never be gauged by cash. Others may give larger sums, for it is easy to sign a check if one has plenty; however, none can have a larger appreciation of its true worth than I.'

In response to this appeal, Tryon sent the man two pictures upon which he set a nominal price. The minister was delighted with them, and the incident established a lasting friendship and correspondence.

Though Tryon was very kind-hearted and sympathetic with those less successful than himself, and remarkably tolerant of the visionary, the impractical, and the improvident in his own profession, he was impatient of bores and very sensitive to the attempts of those who tried to exploit his reputation or impose upon his good nature. Potential friendships sometimes came to an end in this way. An artist in whom Tryon became interested in his early life sent a picture to an exhibition, where Tryon was a member of the jury. The picture was not hung and the artist wrote an unreasonable and insulting letter to Tryon taking him to task for its rejection. Tryon never forgot the incident or forgave the artist. 'I voted for his picture when it came up,' he said, 'but the majority voted against it. I did all I could for him and was not responsible for the picture's rejection.' Many years later the artist evidently regretted his fit of temper and wrote a letter apologizing to Tryon and asking if he would not renew the friendship. Tryon disregarded it. 'I do not wish to

126

be unfair to him,' he said, 'but he spoiled the possibility of a perfect relationship.'

I think Tryon sometimes gave the impression of being unsocial, because he was jealous of encroachments upon his time. He did, indeed, often seem elusive and hard of approach. If you desired pleasant relations with him, a very good way to obtain them was by the well-known method of achieving happiness. Pursue it and it flies from you, retreat and it follows you. It was well to err on the side of letting Tryon pretty much alone. If he liked you, you were never left in doubt. He sought you out and you could have as much of his society as you wished. A friendship once established, neither long absences nor seeming neglect mattered on either side. Barring intrusion on his working hours he was always glad to see his friends, and while his visits to you might be infrequent, when he came the event was memorable. Tryon was not only easy to live with, but most inspiring in every way, in his interests and enthusiasms.

Like most people of strong character, however, he had a sharp edge. And his fundamental honesty, his sincerity and straightforwardness were sometimes a little chilling to persons of conventional easy-going temperament. People sometimes thought him 'blunt,' as they expressed it. He used to say, 'I am not popular because I speak the truth. I think out loud.' Curiously, however, though his plain speaking occasionally gave offense, I think it more often led to respect and liking. An amusing instance of Tryon's frankness and independence of spirit, as well as of his resentment at the least assumption that he would be capable of cheapening his art, occurred when a man who lived in the Middle West, and who had begun, in a groping way, to collect pictures, wrote him in substance the following

127

letter: 'I have seen one of your landscapes in an exhibition and I like it very much. I would like to have you paint one for me; but I wish to make a few suggestions. I do not want a morning or an evening or a moonlight. And I do not want a picture with any crooked trees in it, or any old stone walls, or broken fences, or one with any sticks, stumps, stones, bushes, or pools of water in the foreground. And the picture must be of moderate size. If you will paint one that conforms to these requirements you can set your own price.'

To any one unacquainted with Tryon and his reverence for his art, it would be difficult to describe his response to this letter. The pyrotechnical display that took place when he read it must have illumined a large sector of Central Park. He sat down at once, in his incandescent state, and wrote a reply that, as he told me afterward, took off both the hair and hide of the unhappy offender. 'I was sure,' said he, 'that I never would hear from him again. Then, in a week or two, I had another letter from him in which he said, "I seem to have offended you. But I have thought over what you wrote about art and it has helped me to understand it. I still feel that I would like one of your pictures and I hope you will send me one."' Tryon had had time to cool off somewhat and the humorous aspect of the affair began to appeal to him; and the gentleman's humility and continued interest appeased him. In a letter to me enclosing the one that caused the disturbance, he says, 'The wonder is that he replied to my letter. It raised him in my opinion that he could take such a lambasting as I gave him and not boil over.' The result of this incident was that Tryon, becoming convinced that his would-be patron was seeking the light, finally sold him several of his pictures.

Tryon loved children and their simplicity always appealed to him. Once when he was traveling, a little girl of five or six in front of him attracted his attention and he tried to make friends with her. But she was shy and ignored his advances. Finally he said, 'How old are you, my dear?' The child drew herself up with the dignity of a matron, gave him a withering glance, and replied, 'I don't know that it matters!' Humanity interested Tryon. Some one, in conversation, referred to an unconventional and peculiar person. 'Yes,' said Tryon, 'he's a crank. That's why he is interesting.'

To me the outstanding trait of Tryon's character was reverence. And by that I mean reverence for the things of the mind and of the spirit. He worshiped nature, he had a broad humanity. He was not religious in the orthodox or narrow sense of the term, but he had a great love and respect for the aspirations of the human soul toward spiritual life, especially for the love of beauty. He often said he could well understand the appeal of the magnificence of the Gothic cathedrals, and of the impressiveness of the ritual of the Catholic Church, as revelations of beauty, pure and simple.

I think my brief presentment of his character here indicates his breadth and tolerance. Though Tryon could be frank, and caustic even, in his comments on what he felt to be pretense or insincerity in contemporary painting, if he could not say a good word he usually said little or nothing. He was not a 'knocker.' I have never heard him speak ill of the work of others with malice or intent to injure. And he was quick to recognize and praise merit wherever he found it.

To write adequately of Tryon's diversions of fishing and sailing would require a volume to themselves. I think the references I have made to them, in different chapters, will give a hint of the important part they played in his life. They were, however, so significant of certain phases of Tryon's character that a brief account of them helps to portray him.

He was a constant fisherman and an expert sailor during all the fifty years that I knew him. The greater part of each spring, summer, and fall he spent in sailing and fishing. And even in the winter, when not occupied with his painting, his mind dwelt upon his sports and he planned and prepared for the coming summer. Old Izaak himself was not a more ardent devotee of the gentle art than Tryon. But while Piscator angled mostly in the quiet reaches of the inland streams of England, Tryon fished in all waters, fresh or salt.

'Turner,' says Thornbury, 'was very fond of fishing; he seldom went to visit a country friend without binding up a rod with his pilgrim's staff. He was an intensely persevering fisherman, too, no bad weather could drive him from his post, no ill luck tire out his imperturbable patience; and here, too, I see reflected his greatness; the body that bore the long day's rain contained the mind that had borne the long struggle to fame. When Turner went to Petworth, he always spent much time in fishing. When he went to revisit the scenes of his childhood at Brentford, or walked over from his house at Twickenham, to visit his friend Trimmer of Heston, he always appeared carrying his rod.'

An excellent description of Tryon. The fondness of these two artists for combining fishing with their painting emphasizes their resemblance to each other. No conditions of weather ever dampened Tryon's ardor; no ill luck ever discouraged him. His appetite for his favorite sport was insatiable. And

130

TRYON CAMPING IN CANADA

from the first his fishing contributed to the success of his art. He must have seen many of the subjects of his early pictures while following a rushing trout brook in spring through open meadows or tangled thickets. No one may say what reflections on nature then came to him, or what problems of art he then solved.

When his roving spirit found the sea, however, the field for his sport was immeasurably extended. As his knowledge of the sea and of the life and habits of its fish increased, he developed his angling and lifted it to the plane of a fine art, analogous in the subtleties of its practice to his painting.

Among the many kinds of fish that Tryon caught, the weakfish or squitteague gave him, perhaps, his finest sport. To Tryon's deep disappointment this prolific fish disappeared from Buzzard's Bay after the year 1913, though not because he often caught six hundred or so, or over a ton in weight, of them in a single summer. And lest you should think him wasteful in his sport, remember that with it he fed a multitude.

Tryon was always alert to discover and try new fishing grounds, different species of fish and varied methods of taking them. In June his Maine guide sent him weekly bulletins of the height of water in the Belgrade Lakes and the earliest day when the bass came into the shallow water to spawn. Once he arrived there to find the other fishermen discouraged by their inability to get a rise. Tryon said nothing, but strolled along the shore closely observant of the feeding bass. He soon returned and tied a microscopic black midge of a bass fly on the tiniest of hooks. The bass took it voraciously and the discomfited sportsmen had to admit grudgingly that it took Tryon to start the season, or, as they said, 'To open the show.'

131

The distance to which Tryon could cast a fly left one with a feeling of insufficiency and amateurishness. I have often regretted that I did not measure some of his casts; but, whatever their length, they were always long enough to reach the place, inaccessible to others, where the largest and shyest fish were playing.

For sheer endurance Tryon put some of the Maine guides to shame. In October, 1897, he wrote me:

'... I had about three weeks in Maine and by all odds the most interesting and exciting trip I ever made. I had three different guides before I got out. I left one of them sick in a camp thirty-five miles from civilization and finally came through with a poor cuss who did not know the way and depended mostly on me to pull him through. The only thing that kept him going was a bottle of rum which I had, but which, up to that time, I had not uncorked. When he mutinied I opened the bottle and all went well.

'All told, I helped pole and paddle over one hundred and fifty miles during the trip and when I got out I felt like an Indian and certainly looked like one, or a tramp. I went into a country opened up for the first time and it was rough and hard enough to suit any one. I had the worst and the best fishing I have ever had. One day I caught over fifty trout from $1\frac{1}{2}$ to 4 pounds each, but much of the time was spent in pioneering and much time was lost because we did not know where to locate the fish....'

Tryon showed the same thoroughness and mastery of detail in boating that we have already seen in fishing. He could always design a racing yacht that was just enough better than the best of his competitors to sail circles around them. Since

132

boyhood his leisure has been spent mostly on the water in boats that ranged from the wooden sink of childhood to the racing or cruising sailboats of his later life, most of them of his own design. He pondered deeply the principles of naval architecture; he admired the marvelous creations of Herreshoff and those of the best designers at home and abroad. Nat Herreshoff, he said, was not only the greatest yacht designer in the world, but he was a great artist as well. I have seen Tryon pass his hand over the sweetly moulded hull of a Herreshoff yacht and say, almost reverently, 'It is like a piece of Greek sculpture!'

Tryon's own designs for his boats were the product of scientific knowledge, combined with his artist's instinct for beautiful form added to the experience of many years. He was not naturally mathematical — 'People say figures won't lie, but I can make 'em!' he chuckled. And though he did not scorn the necessary computations of arithmetic in determining, let us say, the correct weight of lead ballast to cast in a boat's keel, I have known him to guess it within a few pounds. Such an achievement always pleased him mightily as of the triumph of intuition and experience over pure science.

One of Tryon's first concerns, after settling at South Dartmouth in 1881, was to provide himself with some sort of sailing craft to use in summer. His modest means at the time and the development of canoeing by Baden Powell led Tryon to this sport and he bought a small sailing canoe. His enthusiasm over his new toy betrayed him into inviting Dewing, whom he had just met, to accompany him on a trial trip on the Harlem River on a blustering windy day in March. The cockpit of the little cockleshell was only large enough for one person, but Tryon wedged his short legs as far as possible under the forward deck, while Dewing, over six feet tall and weighing nearly two hundred pounds, compressed himself into the scant remaining space, back of Tryon. The voyage ended suddenly when, carrying all sail, as they passed under a bridge a back flaw of wind capsized the cranky vessel off the end of a dock.

As Dewing describes the incident: '... She rolled over completely, upside down. There was Tryon, wedged under the deck so he couldn't move. I fell into the water and swam to the stern of the canoe. I managed to right her up so that Tryon's head came out of water. Then he freed himself and we both hung on to the canoe.

'My first remark was: "Hell, Tryon, is this what you call canoeing?" I said later as we talked it over, "Tryon, you know I haven't been in swimming in twenty years and I laughed to find myself treading water just as naturally as ever!" Well, we held on and yelled for help, and presently a longshoreman, in a great scow, heard us and bore down. He was so excited he ran right over us at first. As we emerged from under the scow, gasping and spouting the dirty water of the river, I shouted to him, "For God's sake, don't do *that* again!" He finally came alongside, rolled us onto the scow, landed us, and directed us to a little beer shop up the street to dry our clothing. The proprietor, an old German, told his daughter to build a fire in a stove in a bedroom and Tryon and I stripped ourselves of everything and stood before it while our clothes were drying.

'Tryon said we must stay until our clothes were dry, but I said I was going home at once, as my wife would worry about me. So the old German gave me a heavy blue woolen undershirt which I put on and my half-dry clothing over it, and I

134

hurried home. Mrs. Dewing looked at me and when she saw the blue undershirt she said, "Why, where have you been? You didn't have that thing on when you left home!" Then I had to tell her...'

Tryon first cruised in his canoe from New York to South Dartmouth. He briefly reviews his trip in a letter written to me in October, 1921, upon receipt of a book I had sent him:

'...I shall read "The Golden Parrot" with much interest, as it is the kind of book I always enjoy. Fenger's "Alone in the Caribbean" I liked very much, as it brought vividly to my mind my long canoe cruises alone. While I never made any cruises of such length as his, I found quite enough of interest between New York and Dartmouth, and in spots it was rough enough to give me all the excitement I cared for.

'I don't suppose you remember about it, as it was my first trip here. Mrs. T.... went by rail or boat to Fall River and I started the following day. I sailed out of the Harlem River and took the ship channel through the Sound. I stopped the first night at Stratford, the next at Stonington. I left Stonington early and carried a fresh north wind to Point Judith and found the wind strong northeast there, so I could not make Newport, as the tide was ahead. I did not want to turn tail and run back, so squared away for Block Island, running into the East Harbor. I stayed overnight at the farmhouse where I had spent two summers years before. Next morning the wind was south and I ran over to Newport to get some provisions. I left there after dinner and ran to Westport Harbor, where I stayed overnight. Next day I ran to Dartmouth, where I found my wife waiting for me as I passed through the bridge.

'My canoe was sixteen feet long, thirty inches beam, and

135

carried about one hundred and fifty square feet of sail. Well, it is fine to be young and foolish but it sometimes gets one into queer scrapes....'

Tryon built his first cruising boat, the twenty-four-foot keel sloop Alice, in 1885, and sailed her for seven years. In 1892, he became interested in racing and bought the Herreshoff twenty-one-foot fin keel racing sloop Vaquero, a prize-winner in her class in hotly contested races at Newport and in other racing events of those years. This boat he sailed and raced with keen enjoyment for a couple of summers. Then, in the winter of 1893, he designed a racing catboat, the Vera. She proved unusually fast. Tryon won so many races with her around New Bedford and South Dartmouth that he was finally barred from entering most of them, as the Vera was not only the fastest boat in her class, but she also outsailed many of the larger craft.

Tryon sailed the Vera for five years, and then sold her to a yachtsman who took her to the head of Long Island Sound, where she again won many races and maintained her reputation for great speed. Following her sale in 1899, Tryon owned successively several catboats. In 1915, he designed and had built his last catboat, the Skat, in which he sailed and fished until 1924, the year before his death. She was the ultimate product of his long experience and a perfect instrument for his purposes. As the years went by, Tryon sailed and fished more and more alone. There were few congenial spirits left who shared his enthusiasms or who fitted into his scheme of life and daily habits. Mr. Raymond Fitch, one of his brothers-in-law, sometimes went with him, but for many days at a stretch he had no companion.

The Skat was a centerboard catboat, twenty-one feet long, easily handled by one man. She had a small cabin large enough

136

SLOOP 'ALICE' IN 1885

for a single berth. In the cabin hung an assortment of rods and tackle for different kinds of fishing, and there was a book or two on the shelf. Tryon's usual routine was to take his lunch and stay all day upon the water. Sometimes in light airs he would run in shore and anchor and go below to lie down to read or take a nap. For ten years this boat was his home in summer days.

In 1898, Tryon designed a fine cruising sloop, the Daphne, for his friend Bell. He also made plans for some racing V-bottoms or skipjacks, small seventeen-foot cat-rigged craft for the boys of Padanaram, and in the eighties he designed and built some very successful model yachts, with one of which he won many races, sailing her in the upper reaches of South Dartmouth Harbor against his friend Gifford and other model yachtsmen. So delicately balanced was this model yacht, the Witch, that she could sail herself untouched for half a mile before the wind with a spinnaker set and never jibe, a considerable feat for a model boat. In the fall or early spring in New York, Tryon often sailed model yachts in Central Park on Sundays or late afternoons, when his painting hours were over. One day a lady paused at the shore of the little pond where Tryon was racing his model with the young boys who always found him a congenial companion. She looked on for a few minutes, and then said, scornfully, 'That is a pretty childish occupation for a grown man!' 'Yes,' said Tryon, 'probably it is, but I have seen grown people sit in the house and amuse themselves for hours at a time by playing with bits of cardboard with colored figures on them.' The lady evidently saw the point, for she said no more and passed on.

Loving as he did all processes, both in his art and in his sports, that taxed and developed his skill, the faculties of his

137

mind, eye, and hand, it is not strange that Tryon was not interested either in machinery or in science so far as they destroyed the spirit of adventure. He never owned a motorboat or an automobile. And the obsession of the average mind by these toys amused him. He sat one day on the veranda of the yacht clubhouse at South Dartmouth while two wealthy New Bedford mill-owners discussed their speed boats. 'Bill,' said one to the other, 'you have beaten me this year, but I'll bet you that next summer I'll have a new boat that will take me to Cuttyhunk and back in an hour and a quarter. You will have to go some to beat that!'

'Gentlemen,' said Tryon, 'I have observed your rivalry for several years with interest, and, if you will allow me the suggestion, I think I can save you both much trouble and expense. The quickest of all ways to go to Cuttyhunk and back again is to sit right where you both are on this veranda and not go on the water at all.'

In the fundamental verities of life, its simple homely pleasures, usually accessible and free to all, Tryon found his deepest satisfaction. I think he felt about his work and his play what Whistler says of the implements of art: '... So art is limited to the infinite and cannot progress. A silent indication of its wayward independence from all extraneous advance is in the absolutely unchanged condition and form of implement since the beginning of things. The painter has but the same pencil — the sculptor the chisel of centuries. Colors are not more since the heavy hangings of night were first drawn aside, and the loveliness of light revealed. Neither chemist nor engineer can offer new elements of the masterpiece.'[1]

[1] Whistler: *Ten O'Clock.*

THE SKAT IN 1919

TRYON AT HELM OF THE 'SKAT' IN 1919

XI

TRYON'S FRIENDS

WHEN Tryon took his first studio in New York, he had for neighbors the artists I have mentioned in a preceding chapter — Dewing, Faxon, Low, Gifford, Sartain, and Edwards. Of these Dewing was one of the most intimate. It seems rather singular that chance should have brought together at the outset of their careers two men whose work had such kinship, and who, each in his own province, were to arrive at such distinction. For, more than any two painters I can think of, Dewing and Tryon perfectly and delightfully balanced, supplemented, and reënforced each other in their art. Dewing is to figure painting what Tryon is to landscape. Dewing's women are of the same world, physically, spiritually, and artistically, as Tryon's trees and meadows. With all their fragility and ethereal beauty, their anatomy is as strongly felt as that of Tryon's rugged pastures. The charm of both artists is based upon science and is highly intellectual. For a number of years Mr. Montross held exhibitions of their pictures in which they were about equally represented. No combination

139

of figure and landscape painting could have been more sympathetic and harmonious.

I once said to Mr. Dewing, 'I think one reason why you paint women so beautifully is that you understand them.' But, with his usual perversity, he would have it otherwise. 'No, no, no! All I ever did was to insist that my model should have brains!' This, I think, would well apply to Tryon's choice of subjects, in nature, for they all express a thought, they are not inanimate.

Each artist deeply appreciated and admired the other's work, and this, with certain other elements, formed the basis of their lasting friendship. In their habits of life and their diversions, however, even in their individual tastes and preferences in other art than their own, they were rather sharply contrasted. Dewing was by nature urbane. He was, more than Tryon, a part of the social and artistic life of New York, for there remained always in Tryon, notwithstanding his city residence, something of the provincial. The two had a way of growling at each other that was very diverting, their friendship being equal to sustaining differences of opinion in minor matters. Dewing, for instance, painted mostly on canvas, Tryon nearly always on wood. Neither could convert the other. So Tryon would say to me, after they had argued this question, or some other, 'Dewing is too conservative, in fact, he really is pessimistic!' The next time I saw Dewing he would begin, 'You know Tryon has been down to see me, and he is the same old pessimist, the same little old Yankee nut that he always was!' And again, when Tryon showed Dewing his beloved Blakelock, one of his most precious treasures, with its low-toned somber sky, and hoped, perhaps, that Dewing would feel something of his own

140

enthusiasm for it, Dewing only squinted askance at it and sighed, 'Oh, yes! I had a sky that went bad, too, just like that!' I relate these incidents not alone because they are amusing, but because they show that the friendship of the two men was founded on a basis of truth and reality as uncompromising as the truth and reality of their art. Their common heritage of New England traditions and their understanding of the country and its people made them sympathetic. Tryon also greatly admired Mrs. Dewing's painting of flowers. He called my attention to her work when I first studied with him, and often commented on its exceptional qualities. In fact, he considered her one of the greatest of flower painters, ranking well with Fantin Latour.

Dewing and Tryon had enjoyed together their experience with Freer, and the fact that fine groups of their pictures were hung in adjoining rooms in the Freer Gallery in Washington, in company with Thayer and Whistler, I think, gave satisfaction to both of them.

Tryon and Thayer were also close friends. In their student days in Paris and in their summers in the French country they were much together. They were both idealists of the highest type, both very reverent in their attitude toward their art, and both very much alike in the quality of their imagination. Each of them had a strongly religious nature, although they were too liberal-minded to be bound by creeds or dogmas. They were wont to philosophize together about problems of art from a lofty standpoint and with great seriousness. In the later years of their lives they did not see each other often, but when they did they embraced affectionately, and recalled the happy experiences they had shared in youth.

141

Thayer, unlike Tryon, was the typical dreamer, absent-minded and oblivious of the lapse of time and of his surroundings when he painted. Tryon used to describe a call he made one evening upon Thayer and his wife in their Paris studio. Thayer started a conversation on painting. After a time he said to his wife, 'Why, Kate, I don't believe we have had any supper, have we?' And his wife replied, 'Why, no, Abbott, I don't think we have. And come to think of it, we didn't have any dinner either!' Whereupon they began to rummage about and, having collected some odds and ends of food, brewed some tea and concocted a makeshift meal.

Once Thayer and Tryon were both on the jury of an exhibition of the Society of American Artists. As usual they got into a discussion of art. This time they were debating the effect upon the world if all the works of a great man were destroyed. They stood in front of one of Thayer's pictures. It had a high light in it which caught Thayer's eye as they talked. He lighted a match to tone down the light with its coal. Absorbed in the conservation he forgot the burning match and singed his fingers. Three matches in succession were lighted with the same result. Finally, as the last match scorched him, he exclaimed, 'What the devil am I holding this match for, anyway?'

There were but two letters of Thayer's among all which Tryon gave me to transcribe. Even these are fragmentary, but the one I quote here gives us a glimpse of Thayer's trend of thought and theories of art:

'... A work of art is absolutely a blossom, a flower like all other flowers. Does any amount of horror and decay in the soil beneath threaten to smirch the dewy crystal flower that bursts

142

into life as the summit of the plant whose roots are actually entwined with the hideous ruin in the ground below?

'The cry of to-day for truth is merely the sincere cry of a world that is having its investigation period, and inasmuch as a part can never understand the whole, the world will again realize this impossibility and again become reverent and again have art and religion. To-day our utmost use for angels is to help us "investigate." It is the fatal revelation of our condition that our highest praise now calls art "expression." In the past it was the rendering of un-understood worshipped things and according as it was a great work of art, this attitude of its painter, having executed the command of a Power above him, was obvious. Among the concomitants at least are the causes of to-day's art conditions. The inevitable dawn of individualism has had a great space. Where of old each young artist began with a job at helping some great one make a beautiful and worshipped picture, to-day a hundred youngsters a year pass through each perfectly worshipless painting school in the hope of coming out fitted to cut a figure in our scrap for prominence.

'Worship and art are a period of looking upward into, of course, the infinite. What else do we see when we look on that condition? The looker upward then looks without a dream of understanding necessarily. To-day our eyes are turned down and grubbing with a sneaking hope of getting to the bottom of things.

'Such an attitude is as hopeless for art as it would be to shoot straight backward from a lightning swift express train, and hope to hit as hard as if you shot forward.

'Here, in fact, is the logical goal of Realism; the Strauss vibrationists and all the rest.

143

'The perfected phonograph will supplant all music, since, of course, only a phonograph can perpetuate the million details of passing sounds. Strauss's best reproduction of the sound of frying doughnuts and the spanking of babies will be utterly and finally dispensed with.

'Perfected color photography, sure to come some day, will complete the function of moving pictures and, together with these records of action, sound and color and some smell-record will easily develop, will utterly supplant all literature, all painting and all music, because they will obviously better do everything that the realists suppose to be the objects of these arts.

' ... I would not believe any real artist who said he was trying to express himself even if for want of good analyzing power he thought so. I should be sure that every one of his successes was a thing that haunted him. He knew not why or whence till he obeyed and tried, at least, to set it down.

'Now, at last, the present Strauss's in so-called music and the successes of Monet in paint turn up trying to be cameras each in his way. Strauss is said to be able to reproduce every happening of daily life in music! Are there not happenings enough already if that were all? The same with the Tarbells, though in Tarbell himself something better is at work, deep in, if he could live forty years more. What, if they could make it seem that on their canvas one more man or girl just like the million others loaded like the rest with all the moment's accidents really sat there?

'When Strauss can make great music tell anything he pleases, what a responsibility on poor Strauss! Think what a boast that you have captured the archangel Michael and got him

144

trained to shovel dung or sell cigars equal to any dung shoveler or cigar seller on the street!

'Conceive the triumph when the adagio of the Ninth Symphony could prove to be an accurate inventory of the sounds and the smells of cooking a dinner!

'As for the liberty claimed by these wretches who call themselves Cubists, etc., to spit in the public's face, I fancy that they are partly crazed by the boredom at the camera crowd.'

One day, while sailing model yachts in Central Park, Tryon found he had for a competitor a tall, fine-looking young man with a light blond complexion and full beard who was sailing a model yacht about the size of his own. It was the artist, Benjamin R. Fitz. As the racing waxed keen, the two men became involved in an argument upon the relative merits of different forms of hulls in their resistance to the water and the effect upon their speed. Tryon claimed that a hull with the greatest beam a little aft of the midship section was the faster. Fitz said the advantage was in placing it a little forward. To prove it they made two small hulls embodying the principles and towed them from the ends of a balanced yoke in a bathtub. The experiment proved Tryon to be right. Tryon and Fitz became warm friends, and when Fitz died in 1891 at the age of thirty-six, Tryon mourned him as a friend and deplored the loss to American art. For he considered Fitz one of our most gifted painters, and asserted that had Fitz lived he would have made a great name for himself. When Fitz's pictures were sold at auction after his death, Tryon wrote a short article about him for the catalogue, and he purchased a number of Fitz's best pictures for the collection at Smith College. Fitz and Tryon

145

were particularly congenial because of tastes in common outside their painting, for Fitz was also a fine sailor and cruised in the Peconic Bay in summer in a sloop on which he lived.

Edward A. Bell was another of Tryon's artist friends. Tryon admired Bell's figures, and for many years they exchanged weekly visits to each other's studios, when they were in New York. Tryon designed a fine cruising sloop for Bell, who shared his fondness for the water. Bell has often commented to me on Tryon's remarkable critical ability, which was no doubt developed and intensified by his many years of teaching. Bell said that, more than any artist he ever knew, Tryon had the faculty of almost instantaneously pointing out the one thing that was at fault in a picture, an exceptional critical gift of Tryon's that I have not, perhaps, sufficiently emphasized. So it was that Tryon's artist friends found his visits very helpful. His criticisms always went deep. They were relentless, and often called for radical changes. But he was equally quick to see good. He entered heartily into the spirit of what you were doing, and when he praised your work, you knew he was sincere. A call from him was always inspiring.

Tryon also esteemed very highly the work of George Alfred Williams. They found, at their first meeting, that they had much in common, in their art and in their love of nature, and they kept up an interesting correspondence from the time they met until Tryon's death. With artists who, like Mr. Williams, had literary interests, in addition to their painting, Tryon was very congenial.

In the enjoyment of literature there was no one with whom Tryon was more in sympathy than the architect E. K. Rossiter, of New York. To be present at one of their meetings was an event to be remembered. Each had a remarkable memory for quotations and for books they had read. The conversation was sparkling and witty. Rossiter also greatly admired Tryon's painting. It was he who designed Tryon's South Dartmouth home. Mr. W. K. Bixby, the connoisseur, was Tryon's friend. Professor Bickmore, of the Museum of Natural History, was a neighbor in the Harperly Hall Apartments. They were drawn together by their interest in nature. They became warm friends. Dr. Leroy M. Yale was another intimate friend of Tryon's. He was an etcher as well as a physician and as fond of fishing as Tryon. Victor Harris, the composer, too, was a patron and personal friend.

Others found their way into the charmed circle simply through Tryon's response to fine personality. Those, too, who had a deep love of nature held the key to his sympathy from the start of their acquaintance. The quotation from the letter of the Reverend J. A. Donald, in an earlier chapter, sufficiently illustrates my thought.

XII

TRYON'S ART

In considering the art of Tryon we have to deal with two qualities distinctly different, if not opposed — the ability, as an accomplished technician, to record facts, and the insight that uses facts creatively as symbols of a higher truth. We often find in the work of a skillful craftsman a cleverness that excites our admiration, but whose charm is shallow and impermanent because his art is not the vehicle of imaginative feeling. And, conversely, the art of many painters, usually classed as imaginative, often fails to convince because it has too slight a relation to reality.

And it is here that we must distinguish between the true creative imagination that is able to invest with poetry the familiar scenes of earth, those universal symbols, visible to us all, and the vastly inferior talent which depends upon mysticism or adventitious literary aids. Emerson states in 'The Poet' that mysticism consists in the mistake of an accidental symbol for a universal one. It seems to me that Tryon was one of those rare geniuses who selected with sure grasp the material

148

which Nature offered and transformed it into visions of universal significance. I have seen him reproduce, upon the two dimensions of a painted surface, the very *processes* of Nature herself. He would first paint a scene of spring or autumn that fully realized the clearness, the complete detail of midday. Then, enveloping his forms with veils of transparent pigment, just as Nature with her mists enshrouds them, he would induce the mood of dawn or twilight.

'People think of atmosphere,' he used to say, 'as somehow less real than the other facts of Nature, but to the painter it is simply a more subtle truth, which he can no more disregard than the rocks in his foreground.' But this pursuit of subtle atmospheric *nuances*, which carried Tryon so far, never diminished his relish for the solid earth. In this he seems to me almost unique among landscape painters.

We have seen in our time how far away from solidity of structure Impressionism, in its exclusive occupation with problems of light, has often led its votaries. Yet, on the other hand, we feel the limitation of those painters who are too exclusively occupied with the rendering of material facts. In Tryon we find the rare and happy combination of the poet and the realist. He preserved, as few have ever done, the just relation between earth and sky, between matter and spirit. The blue thread of smoke that, in his autumn landscapes, fuses and harmonizes the two elements suggests a symbol of his temperament.

Strolling across the bridge at Ogunquit on our return from the beach, one evening, we faced a group of fish houses, under old willows, massed against the glowing sky, and reflected in the quiet water of the river. It was an effect I might describe

149

as the obviously picturesque. 'Charming, isn't it?' said Tryon, 'but,' he mused, 'not a subject for me. I know enough to let such things alone now.' A puzzling remark, perhaps, to any one not familiar with his attitude toward nature, but it implied and included the whole range of his development. As time went on he had wholly abandoned the painting of the conventionally picturesque, the obvious subject. The poems of his maturity were purified of all that.

It was a second of time, a passing phase that interested him. What enthralled him was the memory of those divine moments when Nature throws a spell of enchantment over dusky woodlands at evening, over sapphire sea or golden strand, fleeting visions never to be recaptured. Yet, his desire was for the eternal vision. But that vision must be rooted in reality. 'Whatever else my picture may be,' he used to say, 'it must be true.' By which he meant that it must ring true to the fundamental laws and verities of nature. It must rest secure upon that solid structure, though he might veil the stark reality with the very stuff that dreams are made of.

Tryon's attitude has often reminded me of a saying of Thoreau, 'If you have built castles in the air your work need not be lost, that is where they should be. Now put the foundations under them.' On the other hand, any hint of literary suggestion, any mixture of an alien art, vitiated painting for him and aroused his antagonism. 'When I painted my picture, "First Leaves," I thought of calling it "Resurrection," but I did not, as I do not like literary titles.'

I cannot emphasize too strongly the sanity and balance of Tryon's character in its relation to his painting. I was continually impressed by the fact that his success was largely due, not only to his creative energy, but also to his admirable sense of proportion, his poise and self-restraint. His was preëminently the *mens sana in corpore sano*. He started in boyhood with the inestimable advantages of an iron constitution and perfect health. He drew upon these to their full capacity; but he wisely conserved them. He worked hard at his painting, he played hard at his sports. And he so alternated them that each supplemented, reënforced, and balanced the other.

The hardy life of the sailor, fisherman, woodsman, and camper that Tryon lived for the half of each year reduced painting for the time being to an avocation or diversion. No artist ever revered his art more, or applied himself more closely to it, when the garnered memories of spring, summer, and autumn, spent afield or afloat, clamored for expression. Each April, however, with the regularity of clockwork, he transformed himself from the sedentary worker at the easel, immured in the sophistication of a highly civilized life in the largest city in the world, into a primitive man who wrestled with the elemental forces of Nature. These gave fresh stimulus to his creative impulses, and, like Antæus, falling to earth, he arose with strength renewed.

In an essay called 'Some Imaginative Types in American Art,' [1] Mr. Royal Cortissoz, writing of the three artists Dewing, Tryon, and MacMonnies, says:

'Mr. Tryon has not, any more than Mr. Dewing, sought to devise a complex, an esoteric work. He has preferred to do in landscape what Mr. Dewing has done in *genre*, to interpret nature with absolute simplicity, but with imagination, with subtlety refined to the furthest possible point. The point he has

[1] *Harper's Magazine*, July, 1895.

reached up to the present time is fruitful of no quality more striking than that which he shares with Mr. Dewing, his independence of picturesque convention cultivated for its own sake. The dramatic fire which so often bore George Inness on to a brilliant climax subsides or is altogether absent from Mr. Tryon's landscape. It is his belief that true art never enforces itself upon the beholder but drifts as quietly as it does irresistibly into the mind. The theory would be inferred from his work, of which the principal characteristics are repose, suavity, moderation, and the gentle key of color synthetized to a tone as pure as it is transparent. The synthetic quality is perhaps the most remarkable in Mr. Tryon's work, for it has nothing in common with the excessive breadth of impressionism, and even differentiates itself by an extraordinary delicacy from the admirably solid naturalism which the Fontainebleau men introduced. He has masses in his pictures as may be seen from the grouping of the trees in his 'Dawn — Early Spring,' yet he emphasizes the dictum that art gives you a vision of facts instead of the facts themselves by lifting his masses out of the realm of dense ponderable things. He secures, I think a veracity of vision, of feeling, as distinguished from a veracity of direct contact. The same is true of any thorough landscapist; it is true of many of Mr. Tryon's countrymen; but his pictures are so consummate in this particular that he stands almost alone.

'His technical merits have often elicited the admiration of his colleagues. There is no more complete painter's painter in America to-day. Yet with the same quick and profound sensitiveness to what is finest in art that has been pointed out in Mr. Dewing, he leaves, less than most landscapists, a margin for delight in his brushing and workmanship, his modeling or his perspective. I do not mean that these things are unimportant in him. They are of account in the achievement of his aim. But the first consideration of that aim is to awaken the sense of Nature's living loveliness, the sense of quivering grass and palpitating clouds, the sense of trees that feel the wind, although they do not bend beneath its weight. Executive adequacy is tacitly assumed when these impalpable truths are pursued, and it is with the impalpable that Mr. Tryon is almost exclusively concerned. This might easily be construed as a fault in him, for thinness lies that way; but as a matter of fact, he escapes the charge of tenuity by remembering that the truths of nature are, after all, rooted in the solid earth as much as in the circumambient air. He has therefore not only the flamelike tremulousness which shakes the grass in the foreground of his 'Dawn,' he has also in that, and in all his pictures, the organic equilibrium and depth which speak of close observation, and a sense of the massy structure in wood and field.

'If this structural side of Mr. Tryon's work is not aggressive, not conspicuous in its effect, it is because of his entire freedom from academic habits, his reliance upon instinctive rather than formulated rules of composition.

'It is an old saying that the greatest art is that which conceals art, and it is in the spirit of this adage that Mr. Tryon works. Impressed and satisfied by the strong integrity of his design, one comes back, nevertheless, to the more elusive qualities which engaged our attention at the outset. One ends, as one begins, by praising Mr. Tryon for a synthetic gift which becomes more and more as you analyze it a matter of feeling, of inspiration, and less and less a matter of craft. He must be granted, I repeat, the deliberate fashioning power of the

153

artist; but when you seek the bloom of his art, the sap that nourishes it and the beauty that it sheds, this question of form sinks into its proper relation, and the imaginative impetus of the painter comes to the front as the primal source of his power. This is reiterated because, as was stated in glancing at Mr. Dewing's work, it is for the slow but sure establishment of the imaginative principle that he and Mr. Tryon are to be especially thanked. They prove the great cardinal fact that, given a perfect balance between spiritual and technical qualities in a man's art, it is the higher of the two which goes swiftly to our consciousness and there refreshes and delights.'

Those who are not familiar with the whole range of Tryon's painting will doubtless think of him as distinctively, perhaps almost exclusively, the painter of dawn and twilight. We naturally think of an artist in the phases of his art which are peculiar to him alone. As Northcote, in conversation with Constable, said, 'It should be the aim of the artist to bring something to light out of nature for the first time. Something like that for which, in mechanics, a patent would be granted, an original invention or a decided improvement.' [1] But, although Tryon will probably be remembered as the first of our artists to render with such poetic feeling the crepuscular effects of New England landscape, it would be almost as great an injustice to neglect the other phases of his art as it would be to ignore the figure subjects of Corot.

Tryon did, indeed, portray the tenuous, the elusive and transitory moods of daybreak and of sunset for almost the entire period of his artistic activity. But by no means exclusively. If his art was limited in a certain sense, within its

[1] *John Constable, the Painter*, by E. V. Lucas.

154

limitations it was more varied than perhaps is generally under-stood. His mind was restless and inventive. He continually experimented, not only with the exposition of those phases of nature by which we know him best, but with other and varied themes, less familiar to us. These show a versatility with which he is not always credited. And I shall have occasion to show in a subsequent chapter that he constantly made use of every known and unknown process of technique. These also varied his style and manner. Furthermore, he was so wholly obsessed with the interest of the subject in hand at any given moment that it seemed for the time being to obscure or ex-clude everything else. In his earlier years he said to his friend Bell, 'I don't like to paint the autumn. It makes me think of death.' Yet in later life he spent much time upon a distin-guished series of autumn landscapes. Intermittently, over a long period, Tryon would write or say to me, 'I have practically given up the medium of pastel. It is too fragile.' But at the end of the year I would discover that he had completed another group of pictures in this medium, carried a step farther than any he had previously done. I mention this apparent con-tradiction to illustrate the diversity of his work.

I think it will be well to note here a transition, not only in Tryon's choice of themes, but also in his treatment of them. Mr. Cortissoz says, referring to Tryon's preoccupation with the tenuous in nature, '... it might easily be construed as a fault in him, for thinness lies that way....' The same writer, in a criticism of the paintings in the Freer Gallery, written somewhat later, speaks of Tryon as follows: '... He suffers somewhat as Whistler suffers, from being held up on a pedestal for all men to see. An artist must have a more or less assertive, affirmative energy in him for that.... Emphasis in Tryon is unthinkable.... There is more of a subjectivity that has been carried too far, so that the juices of nature seem to be threatened, if they have not actually been dried up.'

I think this criticism is just, as applied to certain of Tryon's works which completed the period in which those mentioned belong. And I am certain that Tryon himself felt that, for the time at least, he had sufficiently worked, possibly overworked, this vein. At any rate, in 1919, at the end of about two decades, he turned his attention from those *motifs* with which his name is so essentially identified, and began to paint effects of broad daylight. A procession of rich and colorful landscapes ensued, characterful and impressive in their vigorous realism. Many of them, in fact, especially the smaller ones, suggest the 'crushed jewels' of Monticelli, with the added definition of classic form.

In a letter to George Alfred Williams, in 1923, Tryon writes:

'... The past three or four years I have been entirely engaged in exploiting the mysteries of oil as a medium of expression. I have felt that only a few rare souls have tried to wrest from this medium its possibilities. As large pictures take more time and physical strength than small, I have kept in these experiments to sizes I can see when near and cover quickly. As all the poems I care for are short ones, and the musical passages are never very long, I conclude that there is a reason therefor. As all Art is emotional, it seems that a work to be of the highest order must be struck off at white heat. Then, too, the reactions of colors upon each other are greater when kept in close contact, and I have been interested to observe this fact in issuing different sizes. The result of my experiments has been the com-

156

AUTUMN MORNING

pletion of about thirty small pictures in oil in the past three or four years, and all who have seen them think they mark a new phase of my work and that they are big pictures though small in scale. I have given as much time and thought to a panel of 8×12 as I would if it were ten times the size. From these experiments I have learned some things in the use of oil that I am carrying out in larger work — $20 \times 30 — 16 \times 24$. This explains why I have neglected pastels and why at present I have none on hand.

'I find all my life I have worked in this way — some dominating idea seems to rule me and I work with great interest until I feel I have worked out the problem. It then ceases to hold me and seems to become a part of my general system of expression. I am then ready for a new effort and in this way the art of painting is ever new and vital. The trouble with most artists is that they seem to feel that their art, or at least their technical method, has a definite end, and when they achieve a certain success they rest satisfied.'

As I write I glance up at one of these later pictures of Tryon's which hangs upon the wall. The subject is an autumn pasture, clothed in rich browns and reds, with two stately oaks as the principal objects in the composition. Over the whole scene cloud shadows and sunlight play. The sky moves swiftly and torn masses of vapor scud across it, opening, in the central passage, to reveal a glimpse of turquoise blue. It is the aspect of daytime, to be sure, but a daytime dramatic and stirring, and invested with the cool, breezy, and invigorating thrill of late autumn, in all the glory of its rich and mellow color. The size, too, of the picture, which is twenty by thirty, lends it dignity and impressiveness.

157

Beside this landscape hangs another, painted during the same period, between 1920 and 1925. It is also an autumn subject, but wholly different in spirit. This little panel, which measures but nine by twelve inches, presents a bit of level meadow, where the warm greens of summer still linger, but where the early frosts have touched the bushes with scarlet. In the middle distance are misty trees against a hillside. The sky, in tones of gray and gold, is clearing, and the sun is struggling to break through the mist. The atmosphere fairly drips with the moisture of the rain, just passed. In this last series of Tryon's autumn pictures, to which these belong, the effect is always varied. Each is distinctive and unique in sentiment, in design, in color, and in handling. As he often said, each picture was a new problem, and he never felt or painted two in the same way.

One of Tryon's finest pictures is the magnificent 'Night — New England,' owned by Dr. F. Whiting, of New York. This noble moonlight might, perhaps, stand as Tryon's masterpiece. In fact, Dr. Whiting has quoted Tryon as having said of it to Dr. (T. L.) Bennett, 'If I could recall every picture that I have painted during my lifetime and select one for my own possession, this is the picture I would choose.'

To those who know Tryon only by his easel pictures his ability as a decorator would scarcely be suspected. He had the talents of the true mural painter. This is shown by his decorations for Freer's house in Detroit, now in the Freer Gallery in Washington, and by several other large decorative works. Among them may be mentioned the 'May,' owned by the Carnegie Art Institute, and 'The Brook in May,' formerly owned by William A. Rogers, of Buffalo, now in the collection of the writer.

158

MORNING MIST. OCTOBER

There is a cardinal principle of mural decoration which comparatively few artists commissioned to execute these works seem ever to grasp. It is this, that, in a general way, the larger the surface to be covered, the paler and quieter the color should be, the simpler and more severely dignified the form. An easel picture up to the size, let us say, of twenty by thirty inches may glow and sparkle with the richest, deepest tones that can be mixed with pigment and still be agreeable. But, let these tones and colors be expanded to cover a large wall space and they lose their preciosity and become vulgar. Any large canvas should, in reality, be considered a mural decoration. If it is to keep its place on the wall, the color should be sober and restrained, the planes flat, and with but slight suggestion of modeling.

These principles are nowhere so well demonstrated as in the masterly murals by Puvis de Chavannes in the Sorbonne and the Panthéon. Their superb and classic design, their pale and delicate loveliness of color become a structural part of the wall itself. Their perfect fitness and complete success is the more strongly emphasized in the Panthéon by contrast with the works of Bonnat and other French painters which adjoin them, most of which are all that mural decoration should *not* be. A similar lesson is taught by the Puvis de Chavannes designs in the staircase hall of the Boston Public Library. They are so quiet, so unobtrusive, that they are lost upon the average visitor, probably sent by well-meaning friends upon a special mission to view the Sargents and Abbeys upstairs. But here again, and I say it with all respect for the achievement of the latter artists, each in his proper field, these works of Puvis de Chavannes are true mural decorations. The panels by the

159

other men are merely enlarged easel pictures whose relation to the walls is not demonstrable.

I permit myself this digression in order to call attention to a phase of Tryon's genius that might otherwise be overlooked. Any one who views his murals will be convinced that Tryon had an instinctive and rare gift for decoration, a keen sense of both its possibilities and its limitations, and a general feeling for what I will call, lacking a better word, its *rightness*. And strangely enough he seemed able to infuse even the most austerely simple and rigidly restrained of his decorative motives with a large measure of Nature's naturalistic charm. Mr. Montross has told me that Tryon said to him, in one of their talks on art, 'Every picture should be a thought and a decoration.'

Mr. Cortissoz, in the essay from which I have quoted, refers to the Freer decorations:

'For the hall in this house Mr. Tryon executed seven pictures, the largest a canvas of some eleven feet in length, and all of them in the neighborhood of five feet high. I emphasize this question of scale because it bears upon the scheme in which the pictures are arranged. They were all conceived with a view to their final destination; they were all painted as panels in an architectural *ensemble*. Their proportion, in brief, was fixed by the plan and height of the hall. The occasion was here offered, if ever, for a decorative if not purely formal series of designs. Mr. Tryon might have used an academic plan in the work had he chosen. He elected, however — and in the election lies the finest demonstration of his talent — to bring the unity of Nature into the hall rather than to subdue his outdoor inspiration to the hard-and-fast conditions of his space. He did

THE BROOK IN MAY

not pile up his motives in designs that sought to harmonize themselves with the linear elements in the hall — a course that might easily have justified itself in the hands of a master of convention. He endeavored rather to preserve the intrinsic symmetry of landscape — the symmetry that falls instantly into line with the poise of architectural things, irrespective of where the place may be.

'Before me is one of Elbridge Kingsley's masterly wood-engravings, a reproduction of the "Spring Morning" which figures in the Detroit series — a succession of pictures, by the way, devoted to the passage of the seasons. Reduced to the broad simplicities of a monotone, all the structural character of this work stands forth, and how noble it is! It is a lyric moment that is celebrated in this dainty vision of faintly moving, scarcely breathing Nature, with the soft whites of the apple blossoms rendered still more diaphanous by the veiling half-lights of the dawn, but there is something almost stately in the measured lines of the composition. The few erect trees, halfway up the canvas, the inclined apple trees in the middle distance, the thick groves and dark horizon of the straight-ridged hill beyond, everything in the scene is subtly, emotionally interpreted, yet everything is subject to the keen selective eye of the artist, and you feel he has hit upon the æsthetic secret of their pictorial relationship, that he has flung them into just that unified, almost isolated group which Nature herself intended. The details are welded into one spontaneous whole. The effect would not be so fine were it not due to a conscious fusion of varied material. It is because Mr. Tryon is an artist, because he selects, arranges, refines, and finally forms his pictures that he is admirable.'

161

The late Charles H. Caffin, the critic, describes the large decorative canvas called 'Springtime' which gained the gold medal in 1898 at the Carnegie Institute exhibition. It is a picture seventy-one by fifty-eight inches.

'The coarse grass in the foreground is interrupted by a large slab of rock, and similar outcroppings of this barren harvest of some primeval earthshock strew the ground to nearly half the distance of the picture. Here and there is a wiry bush that, like the grass, is fledged with the shrill green of a still chilly spring, and there are four slender trees, whose budding green, however, being faintly dispersed against the sky, shows softer. This rock-strewn patch, so familiar a sight in the uplands of New England, suggesting a graveyard of an extinct phase of Nature, is bordered by a rude wall of piled stones, beyond which lies a stretch of arable land, pale violet-brown, reddened in the furrow upturned by a plough. This fragment of soil, snatched from the wastes and desolation, is separated by the silver thread of a stream from the background of hills, whose green appears almost colorless against a pinkish, palish blue sky, chill and cloudless, but alert with air. Amid the natural austerity of the scene the one human touch is supplied by the distant group of the ploughman and his team. The cool, hard light, diffused evenly over the landscape, permits no contrast of light and shade, and reduces the values to a meager range in a minor key; inviting no illusions, captivating with no surprises, but relentlessly laying bare the naked facts in all their commonplace, average uniformity.

'Yet, notwithstanding this, bit by bit, with the untiring conscientiousness of consummate craftsmanship, Tryon has given its separate characterization to every item of this average

162

assembly of facts; laying step by step the foundations of his groundwork, and building plane after plane the just elevations of the but slightly differentiated distances, till he reaches the sky and draws it forward to invest the whole solid structural fabric with an envelope of lighted atmosphere. It is an extraordinary example of complex and subtle composition, the fidelity of which, as you study the difficulties that it involved, amazes you. But it does more. It presently bewitches you.

'You become conscious of the charm that the technical precision of excellence has wrought. The structure, like Thebes, has grown to music. The rhythm and relation of the values are so discernible that the austerity of the scene melts into melody, its assemblage of inconsiderable items becomes united in harmonious charms, the very air palpitates with song. As the far-off singing of a distant choir, trembling in the sky it faintly stirs the awakening foliage and hovers like a sigh over the earth that after its long sleep begins to be awake. Spring is astir once more, with its first faint whisper of the renewal of life.' [1]

It is not possible to describe in detail many of Tryon's pictures, tempting as is the material from which to select. Nor would it be altogether profitable. After all, words must always seem inadequate to translate the visual charm of great painting. It is helpful, however, to reënforce and confirm my own impressions by the feeling and insight of others. Caffin, whom I have just quoted, also gives us a summary of Tryon's qualities in a given picture that well renders the spirit of them all. He says:

[1] *The Art of Dwight W. Tryon — An Appreciation.*

163

'In his pictures the skies are usually cloudless,[1] the fore-grounds, for the most part, uncharacterized by conspicuous features. They are, in fact, to use a studio term, "empty spaces" in the composition, which serve to set off the middle distance, in which he places the objects of purely local signifi-cance. Yet in the usual acceptance of the term, they are the reverse of empty. These cloudless skies are filled with light; wells of luminous fluidity, into which one gazes to find no hindrance or limit to the onward sweep of one's imagination. Similarly, the foregrounds have a depth of structural reality that makes them seem a part of the foundation of the earth it-self. Nor is their surface unfilled with character. Though they offer few arresting features, they are alive with the thousand and one accidents and surprises of Nature's life. The appear-ance of their visible facts and the consciousness of the under-lying facts of earth and rock structure are realized with quite extraordinary vividness.

'It is, indeed, on the basis of these foregrounds that Tryon invites one to take one's stand and accept his point of view. Under us is the earth's sure firmness, all about us the evidence of Nature's facts, trivial, perhaps, to a careless eye, but, I sus-pect, for that very reason, studied and observed and rendered by the artist because he feels in their very trivialness a symbol of the comparative unimportance of all Nature's visibilities, even the grandest, when viewed in relation to the limitless Invisible. It is from this basis, I take it, of ocular and mental comprehension, that he would have you start upon the ap-preciation of his picture. There, as the eye and mind travel

[1] This, I think, is misleading, in an otherwise excellent criticism, for cloudless skies are the exception in Tryon's pictures.

164

SPRINGTIME

across the foreground and reach the middle distance they gradually experience the change from direct and forcible realization to suggestion. Here, the facts, though no less real, have become less palpable, even less visible; have been divested of much of their concrete significance and have begun to take on something of the abstract. As forms, these trees are already disembodied; they are spirit forms; breathless, motionless, against the spirituality of the sky. One has, in fact, if one treads the path that the picture invites, been led gradually from a realization of the facts of Nature, as we know them, to a consciousness that they are symbols of what we do not know, but may believe in. From purely sense perception we have attained to an exercise of the intellectual imagination.'

Caffin also says in the essay from which I have quoted: 'Tryon's imagination is... intellectual. He is akin to Emerson in the character of his spirituality; with enough of the Puritan heritage of conscience to have no stomach for evasions, however beautiful. He would not transform the vision of the world into a dream, but interprets its temporal and local realities in terms of universal realism. To him... the concrete is a symbol of the abstract; in which respect he suggests an interesting parallel with Ibsen. To Ibsen's mind the larger issues of life were constantly present, and in the light of these he studied the individual instances. His characters are types; but more than typical of a certain range of temperament; they are, in many cases, at any rate, symbols of the universal idea of which the temperament is but a symptom.'

There is somewhere related a saying of Millet's to the effect that there were many French painters who could travel to

Africa and paint palm trees to one who could stay at home and paint an apple tree. Tryon often quoted the little verse,

'Oh, sculptor, take this maxim to thy heart,
Take of that which lieth nearest,
Shape of that thy work of art.'

A gentleman visiting Tryon's studio one day in April was looking at one of his spring landscapes in which the trees were faintly flushed with the tender greens and pinks of bursting leaf buds, a fleeting phase of the season. 'Mr. Tryon,' said the visitor, 'I like that picture very much, but I don't quite understand the trees in it. I don't remember to have seen any just like them.' 'No,' said Tryon, 'probably not. Few people do notice the subtleties in Nature. For the most part they are merely conscious either that the sun shines or that it rains.' A year passed and the same visitor called again. 'Mr. Tryon, do you remember my remark of a year ago, when I said I didn't understand the trees in your picture?' 'I do,' replied the artist. 'Well,' said the man, 'when I left your studio that day and walked across the park, I saw your trees everywhere.'

Somewhere about the year 1890, Tryon became interested in the medium of pastel. The more he worked with the colored chalks, the more possibilities he saw in them, and he ended by producing a series of small pictures in this medium that push it to the extreme of delicacy, of subtle *nuance* of tone and color. Pastel, in fact, has inherent qualities and possibilities that were peculiarly adapted to Tryon's temperament and to the elusive effects, by which we have come to know him. Its delicacy and fragility, its powdery opacity, the very essence of atmosphere itself, a quality almost impossible to obtain in oil, fascinated Tryon. Its comparative impermanence was its only disad-

166

vantage, and this he largely overcame with a special fixative, which anchored the pastel to its ground without perceptibly changing its tone or color.

The series of twenty or more delightful little marines in the Freer collection represent an interesting variation from his work in oil, carried on simultaneously with his pictures in the latter medium. Their titles give a hint of their variety and are in part, as follows: 'The Sea-Evening,' 'East Wind,' 'A North-easter' (a heavy, yeasty sea breaking on rocks), 'Shift of Wind from East to Northwest,' 'The Sea-Night,' 'Drifting Clouds and Tumbling Sea,' 'After Sunset,' 'Before Sunrise,' 'After-noon,' 'Moonlit Sea,' 'Northwest Wind Making Up,' 'Moon-light,' 'A Light Northeast Wind,' and 'A Misty Morning.' The size of nearly all of them was eight by twelve inches. Writing to George Alfred Williams of these pastels shortly after they were painted, Tryon said: 'I brought home with me (from Ogunquit) a series of twenty pastels which I called "Sea Phases" (afterward "Sea Moods"), and which I expected to exhibit at Knoedler's sometime in the late winter, but Mr. Freer saw them and bought almost the whole set, so I will probably not make any show. I wish you might see the collection before it is dispersed, as I feel it represents me at my best, though the works are small in size.'

Tryon never wearied of watching the play of light and color on the sea, in calm or storm. Water in motion fascinated him, and he always said the most difficult thing to render was its movement, that most marines were static. In one of the Ogunquit pastels the moon rises over a sea of deep lapis-lazuli, with but a trace of the sun's afterglow in the eastern sky. The waves break gently on the low-toned sand. It is subdued, like a

167

musical nocturne in spirit. Another picture, diminutive in size, has the grandeur of a great symphony, with full orchestration. You not only see the confused wrack of the storm, but you almost hear the booming bass notes of an easterly gale at its climax, hurling great surges against the rampart of rocks, to recede in seething caldrons of spray and spume.

Some of these little sea-pieces suggested motives for larger pictures, and Tryon painted a number of fine oils, using them as motives. There is one in the Freer collection called 'Twilight Seas.' It is a large picture, but severely simple in its composition and very quiet in color. Writing to Tryon in August, 1907, of its arrival in Detroit, Freer says:

'The big marine came safely night before last, since when I have been "soaking it in." It is a wonder! — Marvelously convincing, tremendously powerful and extremely dignified. Nothing could be more truthful, and at the same time so subtle. I certainly think, that in many ways it is the top notch of all your work known to me. Certainly, I have seen nothing more suggestive of that particular mood of the sea. The coloring is very beautiful and recalls the work of the great masters of the early Kano school — Sesshu, Sesson, and Masunobu. In one of the great Kyoto temples there is an ink painting of a huge waterfall by a painter called Omakitsu. This picture I was permitted to study most carefully on several occasions during my recent stay in Japan, and I believe it to be one of the greatest pictures in existence. You, I am sure, would be fascinated by it. Its great qualities are simplicity, line and notan (light and dark). Color, if added, might have given it additional charm, but it certainly could not have increased its subtlety or suggestion.

168

A NORTHEASTER

'Your marine, while totally different in subject, has, to me, the same big qualities of excellence. I am mighty glad to become its caretaker. Some day you may paint a better one — you surely will if it is within the possibilities. This masterpiece is the outcome of your splendid experience and study. And so long as you continue to study as you do and to live your own life, you certainly must reap the benefit through higher and higher expressions of beauty....'

Tryon's habits of life tended to diversify the subjects he painted. Though he always roamed the country, he sailed and fished so much that his occupation with nautical affairs, which necessarily play an important part in this history, may seem to overbalance his intellectual interests. It is for me to tell of these things as they were. At all events, these influences had much to do with his development, for he began as a marine painter, turning more to landscapes as he advanced. Some have regretted that landscape occupied him mostly during his latter years, so fine were his occasional marines, but whatever the subjects he painted, he decidedly chose the flavor of sea-salt to season his banquet of life. To present him truly we must include that flavor, along with those pungent distillations in his landscapes, the earthy odors, the fragrant incense of New England woods and fields.

I have been asked whether Tryon ever painted or made a sketch of man, woman, child, or animal, whether he ever put people in his works, and if not, why? Was it not odd that a man so trained did not sometimes paint faces or figures, if only for amusement — in a sketchbook? Had he not the slightest curiosity of *motif*? I would answer that he was, indeed, mostly preoccupied with landscapes and marines. The pictures he painted outside of this field are so few as to be almost negligible. He could and did, however, paint the figure, heads, animals, flowers, and still life, not only very competently, but often very beautifully. There are two self-portraits by him, one owned by Smith College and one by the Freer Gallery. And scattered along the years are charming little studies of flowers, a bit of garden, children picking daisies in a meadow, haying scenes with figures of men and horses, cows at pasture, and other variations of landscape.

One rainy day in winter, many years ago, while I was studying with Tryon in New York, it became too dark to paint. He rummaged about the studio and brought forth a great pile of canvases removed from their stretchers, which he gave me to look over. Individually they are dim in my memory. But there were scenes on French rivers with washerwomen on the banks, castles and châteaux, men loading drays with merchandise. There were architectural subjects, the old streets and churches. And, in Holland, bridges spanning the canals, hay barges on the Maas, windmills, and many scenes enlivened by figures and human life. Tryon also made interesting drawings and sketches in charcoal and crayon of Paris, and, in the early years, a good many water-colors. So far as I know, he never made but two or three etchings. He told me that the indirectness of the process injured it for him, and the fact that the proof was reversed, when printed, 'put him out' as he expressed it. He said, too, that he always felt the need of color to arouse his interest.

While Tryon appreciated good figure painting, I think he never cared as much for it as for landscape. He greatly admired the work of his friends Dewing and Thayer, and that of George

DeForest Brush; and he liked the portrait of Henry G. Marquand in the Metropolitan Museum, which he considered to be Sargent's masterpiece, though he did not place Sargent, as a creative artist, as high as he did Thayer. Sargent's technique, flashing and brilliant as it is, never, to him, approached the courageous and varied experiments of Thayer, who was always willing to take a chance with his picture in the striving for finer qualities.

Although Tryon was always interested in new or different points of view, his art was too deeply rooted in the great traditions to be much influenced by revolutionary theories of the moment. Speaking of the claims of modernistic painting, he quoted Albert Woolf, 'The good that is not new, the new that is not good.'

Tryon's art developed as naturally and proceeded in as orderly a sequence toward its goal as the growth of an oak, or the life of a flower from seed to bloom. From simple beginnings it steadily grew with his own development, to its final complexities. And he was reflected in every phase of it. Philosophizing about life he used to say, 'It isn't what you *do*, it's what you *are*.' And when you knew him you felt unmistakably that the integrity of his character and of his art were one. Starting with great natural gifts, but with the invaluable faculty of self-criticism, he strove first, as we have seen, to perfect himself in the technique of his art, to lay a solid foundation in the essentials. To these he added, throughout his life, all that could cultivate his mind and taste and stimulate his imagination. He used to say that when his picture seemed dull to him, sometimes, as he painted, he would turn to the rich glazes of his Japanese potteries and saturate his eye with their

171

unctuous tones, and go back to his picture stimulated and refreshed. He studied the history of painting deeply and assimilated whatever he felt he needed of its best traditions. His art rounds out a great period of landscape painting, and carries the wholesome, honest art of Constable and the quiet poetry of Corot to further refinement. 'Reënforced by a more accurate science' is what Caffin has said of it.

He worshiped Nature, he lived close to her, and his pictures breathe her most subtle aspects, her rarest poetry. And with the inspiration he drew from her went the love and appreciation of abstract beauty, æsthetic perception and discrimination, the sensitiveness of the creative artist. Tryon had the instinctive feeling for classic form of an ancient Greek, the refinement of a Chinese ink painter, the exquisite sense of fitness and good taste of a Japanese. It would have been as impossible for him to paint a picture upon a square canvas, or one that approached that proportion, as to violate any other æsthetic principle. His art was intellectual. He was preëminently a thinker. His comments upon art were always stimulating, always illuminating. I wish more of them had been recorded. Mr. Montross has favored me with a few which I quote at random.

'Beauty is fitness.'

'Art is the sentiment of a thing.'

'The higher the artist goes in music, literature, or painting the smaller the circle will be to which his art appeals.'

'Color in painting is like music, harmony at a proper distance.'

'The quiet, sober notes and color are the finest.'

'The highest technique is not felt.'

'Reserve power is as great in art as in oratory.'

172

'A picture should belong to the room. Start the house from the picture, and build for it. Painting is closely related to architecture. A picture is a thought and a decoration.'

'The impression of the instant is not obtained by painting out of doors because you see something different every minute.'

'Discovery or knowledge of the great laws of nature makes creation possible in art.'

'Mystery, infinity. A painter who feels these truths in nature is humble. He frankly acknowledges there is something that cannot be painted. But this draws him on, and the highest and most lasting things are these suggestions. In this striving for the spiritual, the higher the whole, so insensibly but surely parts come to belong to the whole.'

'... The most beautiful pictures are usually an intelligent combination of more or less abstract things rather than an exact rendering of objects, the quality of the work often depending on the perfect relation of a few tones of color to each other....'

We who are familiar with Tryon's work shall remember him by pictures which, as Mr. Cortissoz has so well said, 'do not overwhelm you, but drift as quietly as they do irresistibly into the mind.' We shall take delight in his renderings of the flush of dawn, the lingering glow of golden evenings, his translation of the evanescent, ethereal passages of spring, and his misty moonlights. We shall feel, in his marines, the grandeur and tumult of storms, the sting of salt spray upon the cheek, the scent of kelp and rockweed in our nostrils. He portrayed even the austere beauty of winter — in fact, he ran the gamut of Nature's moods. He reveals a loveliness and his pictures hold a

173

subtle charm unseen, or seen faintly, except by those of kindred spirit. With his rare poetic and spiritual qualities and his consummate skill as a craftsman, he has produced works that mark an epoch in landscape painting. I believe they will endure with the best art of all time.

XIII

TECHNICAL METHODS

Most modern artists seem to have ignored the significance of the fact that so many of the old masters, especially those of Italy, France, and Holland, painted upon wood panels. Probably one reason is that many of the panels of the olden time consisted merely of a single board of straight-grained oak or mahogany, without backing or reenforcement of any kind. Naturally, in the course of time, by atmospheric changes and the drying and shrinking of the wood, they have warped, cracked, and split, with resultant damage to the picture. Even then it is practicable to have them planed down, the cracks repaired, and, with a heavy cradling, they may be completely and permanently restored.

From long and traditional usage, however, most painters have used canvas. It is far from an ideal material. Its life is limited to about fifty years, at most, at the end of which it is necessary to reline the picture painted upon it, and, preferably, also to mount the canvas securely upon a well-prepared wooden panel, properly cradled. Another and great disadvantage is the fact that any canvas, no matter how tightly and smoothly

175

stretched, is certain, by reason of heat and cold, dampness or dryness of the air, to shrink and swell, and, in time, to show wrinkles; and the slightest wrinkle or unevenness of surface in the canvas destroys the visual illusion of the picture. There are also certain other disadvantageous qualities of canvas, the difficulty of working upon it with vigorous pressure in scraping or other manipulation, without producing holes and hollows; its fragility and constant exposure to danger, through dents in front or back.

In the year 1885 or thereabouts, a manufacturer of built-up wood and veneering in Brooklyn put upon sale a few mahogany and whitewood panels, for the use of artists. They were made of five thin veneers glued together under heavy pressure, with the grain of each layer of veneer crossing the next at right angles. The whole thickness was about an eighth of an inch. Such panels furnish an unchangeable and very sympathetic surface to paint upon and can be grounded in any way, from the grain of the raw wood to a surface like polished marble. And they cannot warp, crack, or split. I have many of them, with or without paintings upon them, which are forty-five years old, which have been exposed to all possible atmospheric changes, and which are still in perfect condition and apparently good for an indefinite time to come.

Tryon, who was always interested in all technical methods and materials, was attracted by these panels and began to use them. He liked them so well that for many years to come he and I both kept a stock of different sizes of them on hand, and used them almost exclusively.

When our stock ran low, we usually put in an order together for about a hundred dollars' worth at a time. The cost was practically the same as that of stretched canvas. The majority of Tryon's pictures, dating from his return from Europe, are painted upon these panels. He rarely used canvas if he could help it, and, if an early picture painted upon canvas was of sufficient importance, he often had it mounted on a panel.

A study of the methods of the painters of the fifteenth and sixteenth centuries, especially in Italy, reveals not only that they used wood panels, but that they grounded them with gesso, producing a surface that is very hard, that does not crack, and which time has proved sound. Tryon liked, at times, to paint upon the raw wood without preparation of any kind. Some of his early pictures, mostly sketches done out-of-doors, show the rich red of the untouched mahogany in the foreground playing an important part in the color scheme. He liked also the dry opaque quality of color which resulted from the absorption by the wood of the oil in the pigment, though subsequently its brilliancy could be restored by varnishing out. He used many different grounds and preparations, but at last usually prepared his panel with a pure white ground. The influence of this ground, he said, was always felt in the picture, to some degree at least, no matter how many the overpaintings and superimpositions of tone and color. It gave a luminosity and vitality not otherwise obtainable.

Occasionally he used a wax medium for his oil pictures. The large 'Dartmouth Moorlands' is so painted, and a few of his larger decorative subjects, among them a spring landscape executed for his New York apartment. And he was much given to experiments with different grounds and papers for his watercolors and pastels. While I was studying with him, he used a rough golden-colored strawboard for some of his water-colors.

He dampened and mounted it on a stretcher, like canvas, and obtained a charming effect by painting with washes of thin water-color in the foreground and distance and using Chinese white in the sky. And when he began to work in earnest in pastel, he was always searching for and trying new kinds of paper. We used to exchange pastel papers and share new discoveries, from those found in wall-paper houses to selections from the stocks of the wholesale paper dealers in lower New York. The conventional pastel paper of ancient manufacture, a sort of fine-toothed sandpaper, Tryon never used. Most of his pastels are done upon the French Ferraguti pastel paper, and his favorite color was a warm grayish brown which seemed to furnish an almost universal halftone for all subjects, as well as being an agreeable undertone of color in itself. Patches and planes of it appear as the local color in the beaches and foregrounds of his small marines.

As his interest in pastel increased, he made trial of different fixatives to give permanence, and found that the one made by Lefranc of Paris, called the Ferraguti fixative, very satisfactory, though he tried one or two others made in this country, with good results. Some artists who have tried to fix pastels complain that the fixative changes or lowers the tone and color. Tryon said that he had used pastel for so long that he could allow for this change and so utilize it that it played its part in the final effect. Some of his pastels were the result of from twenty to thirty different processes of under- and over-working. He would go over his picture with a tone of color and then blow on enough fixative to hold it. Then he would add successive layers of tone and rougher or smoother textures with sprays of colorless fixative between each, until the end. I re-

178

member one picture of good size — about sixteen by twenty-two inches, I think the largest pastel Tryon ever did — upon which he carried this development of the medium, by repeatedly fixing the dry chalk, to a point where, at first glance, it resembled the rich impasto of oil paint. The lights in it were so heavily loaded that they were a quarter of an inch thick. The effect of this work was delightful. It possessed the richness and depth of an oil, combined with the delicacy and dry powdery atmospheric charm of a pastel.

It was Tryon's *tour de force* in pastel, and I think he never carried another picture in this medium so far. He felt, as he told me, that if one were to devote so much labor to a work and to strive for such qualities, it was more logical to use oil, which, as he said, was after all the best all-around medium, possessing more advantages and fewer drawbacks than any. I describe this experiment to illustrate his inventiveness, his readiness to try any expedient that might further his purpose. To get an interesting and satisfactory result he was willing to force the possibilities in any medium to the bitter end.

In a letter to Mr. Williams, replying to a question about fixing pastels, Tryon writes: 'Since you called my attention to the difficulties of fixing pastel, I find I have become almost insensible to the change that takes place and go right on accepting the changed tone as a basis. I have worked in the medium so long that I have become used to the changes and, just as in oil, I take advantage of tones that are unlike those I started with. Often they are worse and sometimes better than I had planned. It certainly has become a personal method of expression and I am often surprised at the strange ways I adopt to make the medium respond to my feelings.... It has taken me at

179

least ten years of experimenting to reach the results you saw last winter. All you saw were the result of many paintings. Some probably of twenty to thirty separate processes to reach the extreme simplicity that alone pleases me.... While I took interest in the medium many years ago, and did more or less work, I felt that it was too fragile to be worth much attention, and began experimenting in fixing so it might be permanent. I at last got in the way of fixing from the foundation up and could work over and over, thus getting more perfect atmospheric relations.'

To attempt to describe the charm and quality of Tryon's art seems to me even more futile than with most painters, by reason of its deceptive appearance, utter simplicity, and the complete effacement of the footsteps of labor. Here is the art which conceals art. It was my privilege to observe his methods of painting through the greater part of his life, and to note the means by which he eventually achieved some of his finest works. They were cumulative. During his early periods he painted directly and obtained his results by one or, at most, two stages of work. Then, as his perceptions were sharpened and his vision became more penetrating, his manual dexterity kept pace, and he ended by employing strange and unheard-of expedients that seemed fantastic, almost beyond the province and possibilities of pigment.

Here is one of his methods: Starting with the mental conception of one of his important works he set about his task with great deliberation. He grounded a mahogany panel with pure white, that its luminosity might influence in some degree at least all further overpainting. Then he indicated broadly the design or composition in rather bold lines and suggestions of

180

masses. Upon this structure he painted his picture with almost complete details of form and modeling in a violent key of color, forced to the extremity of crudity and brutality. This preparation he allowed to dry for some weeks until it was solid and immovable. Then, when the mood was upon him, he painted over this ground with more delicate color, going over the entire surface, in fact painting another complete though more refined picture upon the first. This he again put aside, and allowed to dry. And this process continued combined with scrapings, scumblings, glazings, and further refinements, until his idea was expressed. Sometimes he traversed the distance, from beginning to end, in a winter, and with each of several pictures, which he kept going at the same time. Painting upon a single picture, three or four years elapsed, sometimes, before the final word was said.

But this deliberate and studied procedure was only one of his many ways of working. Mr. Churchill has described to me a variation of this method: 'He told me in so many words (and you could have knocked me down), "I don't know what I'm going to do. I just take a panel and begin. I lay it in very crudely. Crude rich color all across the panel. I work at it until I'm tired of it and turn it face to the wall. After a few weeks or months it comes out again. I fuss with it some more, cut out a tree here and put one in there. I turn it to the wall again. Out it comes again. At last, *all of a sudden, I know what I want.* After that, *one beautiful tone suggests another still more beautiful*—and I try for that. And so on *until it is all beautiful.*"...'

Tryon usually completed about five or six large pictures each year. His favorite size was twenty by thirty inches, a handsomely proportioned rectangle in itself. And with these a few much smaller pictures eight by twelve or nine by twelve, often pastels. But upon nearly all he spent a very long time.

Tryon used to say that the beholder never gets any more out of a picture than the artist has put in. The truth of this is proved by the perennial pleasure afforded by long association with one of his works. Though he wrought with such intensity of interest upon whatever picture he had in hand that it seemed for the time being as if it was to be his masterpiece, as soon as it was finished he became so absorbed with the next problem that he could not always remember a given work. A friend tried to recall one of his pictures to his memory. Tryon could not place it and said, 'It must have been one of those children I begot in a hurry and then forgot.'

If you are an artist and interested in the technique of oil paint and skillful craftsmanship, a close analysis of the surfaces and textures of Tryon's works will reveal strange methods, involutions difficult but inviting to follow. Tryon has 'put in' much. The work will yield it to you if you associate with it long enough.

John La Farge has an interesting anecdote in his 'Considerations on Painting': 'When a friend of mine, who painted as well as any man of his school in the Paris of that day, came to Millet, to lay all this accomplishment at his feet and ask for direction, "It is well," said Jean François, "and you can paint. — But what have you to say?" ("Qu'avez-vous à dire?")' When you look at one of Tryon's pictures you experience a profound emotion, something far removed from the admiration excited by skillful handling of pigment. But if you have the

182

curiosity of a craftsman in fine handiwork, that is there too, if you search for it; though I think its processes are such that, like the work of Ruysdael, it would be difficult to analyze and almost impossible to copy.

XIV

AN ARTIST'S WAY WITH THE WORLD

THAT the artist is impractical, that his temperament unfits him to deal with business affairs, is an axiom widely accepted. Many people, artists and laymen, collectors and dealers, have commented upon Tryon's exceptional financial success, a success equaled by few creative artists, indeed, and a striking example of what seemed contradictory traits in his character. I think it may be difficult, if not impossible, to convince the reader that it was no chance.

This result of a side of Tryon's nature may seem unrelated to the abstract considerations of his art. But it serves so well to explain his idealism, and bears so directly upon the psychology of selling works of art, that I will offer an explanation of it, not without fear that my words will be received with a skeptical smile. The means that Tryon employed to dispose of his pictures were so simple and logical that I feel quite sure they will not be widely imitated. In the first place, as this narrative has shown, Tryon always made sure of an independent livelihood, earned in other ways than by the sale of pictures. He wished to discharge his duty to society before all other con-

184

siderations, and smile at those carping critics who point the finger of reproach at the visionary and impractical artist.

His bread assured, Tryon was absolved at once from petty worries and anxieties and went about his painting with a happy serenity of mind. He could paint to please himself. Extravagant of time, he could strive for those qualities which have made his work distinguished. 'I have never looked upon my work as a means of livelihood,' he writes to Mr. Williams, 'and I am always surprised when it sells. Painting is in the same class with poetry, and while there are, perhaps, poets who make a living, it seems a doubtful staff to trust.' Possibly the average work of art produced to-day would not lose in merit if the young artist first proved his ability to earn his living in competition with the workaday world by some more prosaic means than painting. The 'staff' that Tryon trusted was teaching. The happy circumstance that he loved and enjoyed his teaching I am obliged to concede to that uncanny thing, his luck.

Now for the second ingredient in his recipe for success. I can give it in his own words. Lounging one day in the Century Club, a group of artists were discussing ways and means of selling their work. What patrons were to be cultivated? What societies to be joined? Finally, one of the debaters turned to Tryon, who until then had said nothing. 'Tryon, what do you think is the best way to sell one's pictures?' 'Well, boys,' said he, 'I think the best way is to paint a damned good picture.' I relate this incident because it helps to reveal Tryon's sincerity of purpose, his respect for his art; and, incidentally, his scorn of the mercenary wire-pullings of a class of practitioners who are more concerned with sales than with quality, with money than with merit.

185

'Paint your picture,' Tryon used to say, 'with no thought of money or reward other than the sheer delight in the work itself. Then, when it is as fine as you can make it, peddle it through the streets. Then take it on your back and hawk it in the market-place if you need money.' The strange and inexplicable fact is that Tryon, having painted the best picture of which he was capable, never had to 'peddle it through the streets.' Like the man in Emerson's oft-quoted essay, Tryon simply did something a little better than anybody else, and, although he did not live in the depths of a wood exactly, humanity wore a path to his door.

One of the greatest satisfactions in one's relations with Tryon was that you could always visit his studio and enjoy his pictures with him in complete abandonment to that pleasure, without feeling that he had the slightest thought of making a sale. I called on him in New York one time when he had just finished a little marine, a pastel. Tryon saw that I was much taken by it and this pleased him. I mentally resolved that I would buy it, but we became so absorbed in conversation about other things that we both forgot the picture, and I was on the train on my way home before I thought of it again. I wrote at once to say that I would like the pastel, and received a reply in which he said: 'Why didn't you say so when you were here? Soon after you left, some one came in and bought it. I'm sorry, for I saw that you liked it. I will paint another if you wish and see if I can get the quality you admire.' It may not sound plausible to some, but I am inclined to believe that this detachment was a factor in his success.

Tryon decidedly kept the two activities, production and sale, in separate compartments; but it would be misleading to infer that he made no positive effort to sell. He was systematic and thorough in his business as in his art. His method was to put out only the very best pictures he could produce. He would not let them go until they satisfied his own severe requirements. He then took pains to see that they were placed where they would do him credit, with the leading dealers in the principal cities in the country, or, in his early life, in whatever exhibitions he considered important. Furthermore, the pictures in his studio were always framed with the greatest care and ready to be shown to advantage. And, without ostentation, he made it known to patrons and dealers whenever he had something of interest to show. Last but not least, the final factor of success as I believe, was this: Tryon had a deep and sympathetic understanding of human nature, a sensitiveness and delicacy of feeling, a reticence rare in these days of commercialism, when the public are bludgeoned into buying what they do not wish or need. I think people felt and liked this quality in him and that it contributed largely to the sale of his work. Tryon loved his art for its own sake. His pictures were his children, and when they went out from his home he liked to think they were in congenial surroundings. One of his favorite aphorisms was that 'there is nothing worse than a misfit picture.' 'Take my picture home with you and see if you can live with it,' he would say to a purchaser. 'If you find it doesn't hold up, you don't want it; and I don't want you to have it.'

To the owner of a fine collection of paintings he said: 'When you have my picture at home, hang it for a time on the wall with your Corot. If you find it doesn't hold its own there, return it to me; for I would then know it was not good enough for you.' Sometimes a prospective buyer, trying to decide between

187

two charming landscapes, would say, 'Which of the two do you like better yourself, Mr. Tryon?' He would smile and reply: 'It is for you to decide. The picture that is for you will probably have its way with you, and it would be wrong for me to influence your choice.'

In the days when Albert P. Ryder lived the life of a hermit in the cobwebbed and dusty back bedroom of a tenement house in West Fifteenth Street, I used to call upon him occasionally. Once I tried to buy one of his gem-like little canvases. My appreciation evidently pleased him and he told me he would like me to have it. But after he had washed the picture's face in a basin of very dirty water, and dried it with a very dirty towel, he stood gazing at it with a far-away look in his eyes, a look of fondest love. He had forgotten that I was there. When I gently recalled him to earth, he turned to me, and, with the simplicity of a child, said, kindly and regretfully, 'Come again next year and I think you can have it, if I find I can do what more it needs. I have only worked on it for a little over ten years.' And when I went out from his room into the noise and confusion of the city streets, Ryder strangely seemed the reality and New York the shadow!

It might be hard to convince those who knew Tryon as a shrewd New England Yankee that he regarded his art in as unworldly a way as Ryder. Yet I believe I am in a position to prove it. To mention only one of many similar instances that I remember, I sat with Tryon one day in his studio in the Gainsborough in West Fifty-Ninth Street, before one of his finest landscapes. It was a large panel of early spring which it seemed he had carried about as far as the possibilities of involved technique would allow. He had worked three years upon it, and

188

at last felt that he could do no more. 'That picture,' said he, 'has been finished several times. I have exhausted every technical device upon it, but until now I have always quarreled with it. You know, when one has brought a thing to the verge of completion, spent years upon it, sweat blood over it, and, very likely, a collector or a dealer stands ready to take it for a round sum of money, it requires more than the courage of the battlefield to attack it again, to work freely and boldly upon it, and risk destroying all that has been done, at a stroke. And yet that is the only way to go far in art.'

Tryon was not in sympathy with concerted efforts to stimulate the demand for works of art. When projects were afoot in New York to promote business by opening new and larger galleries, and to augment sales by advertising and the persuasive powers of dealers, he refused to coöperate. The true interest of art he firmly believed would be best served by rigidly restricting its quantity, improving its quality, and by reducing the number and size of galleries. He maintained that a single picture dealer could show, in a small gallery, all the really important works of a given year, and that the dealer would make money. He always said there was woefully little good art being produced at any time, never enough to 'go round.' Naturally such heresy, frankly expressed, did not tend to make him popular among the propagandists.

Tryon usually painted each year about six large pictures of his favorite size, twenty by thirty inches, hardly ever more or less. In the year that he painted the series of pastels called 'Sea Moods,' about thirty-five or forty in all, he produced few or no oil paintings. I am sure he could have increased his income at any time had he wished, but he never would have sacrificed quality to do it. Collectors and dealers often tried to get his pictures, as they approached completion — 'Good enough for me, Mr. Tryon' — 'But not for me.'

Add to the factors I have tried to enumerate the uninterrupted industry of sixty years of painting, comparative frugality of living, and a keen instinct for good and always conservative investments, and you have the explanation of how Tryon became a rich man.

XV

RECOLLECTIONS

So many of my most interesting and valued experiences and happiest hours are associated with Tryon that I have often felt, in writing this book, that I was reviewing my own life in recording his. We were both born in the same New England city, in the mid-Victorian era, and reared in its rigidly orthodox atmosphere. We both possessed intellectual curiosity and an adventurous spirit that led us to evolve a system of thought and spiritual ideals of our own. When, in time, our tastes and interests had drawn us closely together, we found that we had, unknown to each other, come to virtually the same conclusions about the great mystery in which we are all involved (so far as we had come to any) and that we shared the same philosophy of life.

It was a strong bond of sympathy between us. A person who did not wholly understand either of us, but who was endowed with a certain clairvoyance of perception, once said, after a somewhat pessimistic summary of our personalities, 'They think the same thoughts.' Furthermore, we both had an intense love of nature, and especially, a passionate fondness for the sea, with which we had each made early acquaintance, Tryon at eighteen and I at twelve. And, to strengthen our affinity, we had each drawn and painted from childhood.

We were, in brief, fortunate in sharing more than the average community of interests during our long friendship, a friendship in which our relations were as ideal as any I have ever known. There never was the slightest discord between us, or the shadow of a doubt or misunderstanding. We took each other wholly for granted. It is difficult to select from the flood of memories of fifty years that crowd upon me those that are most significant, that best explain or set forth the extremely interesting personality, the delightful companion that he was. It was a rare privilege to observe his development as a man of genius, and a continual pleasure to associate with him as a human being and a friend. His diversity of interests made him very companionable, for he could talk intelligently and entertainingly upon many subjects. Even artists find it wearisome to talk shop exclusively; but when Tryon did discuss painting, what he said was so pertinent that you found yourself making notes of it afterward. Still, you always felt that his outlook on life was broad, and comprehended much that lay outside his art. From our letters and conversations, and from my notes and diaries, I could easily compile another volume of interesting material which must be omitted from this one for lack of space.

I have noted the circumstances of my first acquaintance with Tryon in his Hartford studio in 1875. I did not see him again until after his return from Europe. Then, in 1885, when he was thirty-six and I was twenty-four, the association began that lasted until his death. He had then passed through his hardest struggles. He was established in New York and had begun to

192

forge ahead in his art. He had come into his own, and he was enjoying life. He awoke one morning and said to his wife, 'I had a horrible nightmare last night.' 'What was it?' said she. 'I dreamed I was back in Brown and Gross.' I, too, at that time, had spent several years in business, and at last, having decided to study art, had passed the preceding winter in Tryon's studio in New York. Summer was now at hand and he invited me to join him at South Dartmouth to sketch and to sail.

The old city of New Bedford had literary and artistic associations, as well as those of whaling. Herman Melville had sailed from there in the Acushnet. Albert P. Ryder was born there. Henry Thoreau visited his friend Daniel Ricketson in New Bedford in 1855, and William Ellery Channing had gone to live there from 1856 to 1858 to help edit the 'Mercury.' There still remain some of the stately old homes in the residential streets, relics and settings of a social scene upon which the curtain has long since descended.

The village of South Dartmouth in the eighties had, on a lesser scale, much of New Bedford's romantic charm. In fact, one lived there in even more intimate contact with the actors in the drama of whaling. And neither the physical aspect of the place nor its inhabitants had changed much in the preceding hundred years.

A lumbering old stage-coach, closed in by curtains, the trunk-rack in the rear upheld by leather straps, and drawn by a mismated pair of horses, made the daily trip to New Bedford, over four miles of sandy, dusty road. If you were so fortunate as to sit with Oliver Barker, the driver, by the time you arrived in the village you were possessed of an encyclopædic knowledge of South Dartmouth's social life for the entire year since your last

193

visit. You knew which whaling captains were away on a voyage and which were at home; what children had been born and what new boats launched. In fact, you were well prepared to meet and greet your old friends. It was another world, another life than that of to-day, and it is difficult to convey its charm to those who never knew it.

That life Tryon and I knew together and we enjoyed it immensely, though, perhaps, rather casually and thoughtlessly, for we took it as a matter of course. How were we to forecast the blight and devastation with which Edison and Ford, America's patron saints, would later desecrate the fair face of Nature? Those days were idyllic and our experiences were rich in material for the weaving of tales of romance and adventure, which even Melville and Dana had not exhausted.

I may have mentioned that Tryon's first cruising sloop was built in the winter of 1884–85. On July 5, 1885, he wrote me: 'The Alice was launched last Wednesday and now lies waiting for spars and rigging. There was more work on her than we expected and as this is a slow country, everything takes much time. I hope to have her ready by the 18th or 20th.... The position of mate and cook of the Alice is vacant, and I shall be glad to see you here when you are ready to come....' This was the beginning of our sailing, cruising, and fishing together that lasted about forty years.

For three summers Tryon and I cruised in the Alice, exploring the remote nooks and corners of Buzzard's Bay. We also usually sailed to Newport at the time of the cup races in August. He was captain and navigator. I was mate, cook, and foremast hand. Shortening sail in rough water on the Alice was strenuous work, whether lying out on the footropes to reef the

194

mainsail on a jumping boom that hung ten feet beyond the stern, or stowing the big jib, when the thirteen feet of bowsprit that projected outboard plotted eccentric parabolas against both sky and water. It was an even chance of getting wet to the waist only or all over. But she was a fine able comfortable cruiser, capable of going anywhere in any weather.

We always carried sketch-boxes, and night usually found us anchored in some unfrequented harbor surrounded by wild country then little known. The landlocked bowl of Quamquisset, just north of Wood's Hole, was one of these, its shores lonely and unspoiled when we first knew them. Here we lingered to sketch and explore. Rolling hills and giant sand dunes surrounded the little haven and the dwarfed and wind-blown cedars, the rich growth of mosses, bayberry bushes, wild-flowers and gray lichen-covered rocks suggested a Scottish moor. But it breathed the true sentiment of Cape Cod. Each morning we ate an early breakfast on the yacht, and, taking our lunch, went ashore to spend the day roaming over this lonely barren bit of Nature which had a grandeur all its own. Here and there among the hills were scattered a few small farms. One gray lowering day Tryon and I were sketching near one of them, when a farmer's boy driving a herd of cows came up and looked over my shoulder. At noon as we ate our lunch together, Tryon asked me if the boy commented on my sketch. I told him that the boy said, 'It looks like this kind of weather.' 'He couldn't have paid you a greater compliment!' said Tryon.

With his love of the sea and affinity for people of striking personality, Tryon naturally formed acquaintance and even close attachments with the captains who lived in South Dartmouth. He knew them well and was friendly with most of the

195

seafaring people in the village. Captain William Henry Howland and Captain 'Arch' Baker, as he was commonly known, played such an important part in Tryon's cruising and added so much to its zest that they merit more than a passing word. Captain Baker was one of the most respected residents of the town. He had been successful in his voyages, had laid by a competence, and lived an exemplary life in one of the neatest of white houses, with the greenest of green blinds, on Padanaram's streets. He was a pillar of the church and did not drink liquor, smoke tobacco, or swear. Nevertheless, we found him a congenial shipmate, at times.

Captain Howland, however, or 'Cap'n William Henry,' as everybody called him, was our boon companion, always sought by us and always responsive. I blush to record that he was the antithesis of Captain Baker. While the latter had mainly commanded whaleships, Captain Howland had sailed the seven seas as master of P. and O. Steamers and tea clippers to China, as well as whalers. His life motto, it seemed, had been 'Wine, Women, and Song.' And the fact that he did not attend church and was free of all prejudice against sailing or fishing on the Lord's Day fitted him well into our scheme of things. A striking figure altogether, invested with a pleasant glamour of romance and adventure. And I am sure you can picture us as we lay below in the cabin of the Alice in some snug harbor at night contentedly smoking our pipes, each with a glass of Tryon's special brew of punch at our elbows, while Captain William Henry spun thrilling yarns of hurricanes and typhoons, until, at length, soothed by the lapping of wavelets against the hull and the tapping of halliards against the mast, we fell asleep.

In the summer of 1886 we made one of the most interesting of our cruises, in some ways typical of them all. Tryon, Captain Howland, and I sailed westward from South Dartmouth to our destination, Rocky Hill, on the Connecticut River, about thirty-five miles from Long Island Sound. We touched at Newport the first day, then on to Stonington, where we lay overnight. Sailing west from Stonington to the mouth of the Connecticut, we made our way slowly up that stream, baffled by calms and the freakish winds of fresh-water navigation. Tryon had relatives at Rocky Hill, and we anchored off an old shipyard there and went ashore to visit them.

After a short stay we doubled on our course and returned to Newport, where we saw the cup races. We lay there for several days while a heavy southeast storm came up. It lasted so long that Tryon being overdue at home became impatient to sail. At the first signs of breaking of the gale he announced that he was going to run down to Brenton's Reef lightship, inspect the conditions, and see if he thought we could make it. It was still blowing heavily and no craft of any kind had left its moorings in the harbor. Captain Howland glanced apprehensively at the storm-clouds and the breaking seas that dashed along the cliffs of Prudence Island, but he said little. We put in all the reefs the Alice had in her mainsail, set the storm jib, stowed our crockery and oil stove securely below, and weighed anchor.

It was a long leg and a short one on the beat to windward to Brenton's Point and we kept close under its lee as the head sea killed our way. Once clear of the land, however, where we felt the full strength of both wind and sea, we found ourselves in the setting of a majestic marine picture.

The little sloop rose and fell between seas that ran to half

197

the height of her mast and shut out momentarily the sight of land. They were so long that she rode easily and she slowly worked to windward. In the south a sickly sun broke through the scudding clouds in gleams of fitful light and to the north the black rack of the lee set was blowing landward. Shortly after our departure, a large schooner yacht also started out. I never shall forget the spirited and thrilling sight of her as she followed us a half-mile astern. She had a close-reefed mainsail, a reefed foresail, and a forestaysail set. Her crew, clad in oilskins, huddled along her windward rail, and as she cleared the harbor's mouth she pitched so violently that when her bow rose to the seas, we could see half the length of her keel from her forefoot aft.

It was grand and awe-inspiring, a dramatic scene, and one which would have appealed to Turner who might have made a masterpiece of it.

As we cleared the shelter of the land, Tryon looked at the miles of stormy sea to the east and said to Captain Howland, who had been rather quiet, like ourselves engrossed in the handling of the yacht, and watching the combers that threatened to board us, 'Well, Captain, what do you think we had better do? Keep on or run back and wait for the storm to blow out?' The Captain surveyed the sea and sky gloomily as he steadied himself in the gyrations of the pitching and rolling sloop. 'Tryon, I don't like the look of things,' he growled. 'It's over forty miles to Padanaram and it's going to get worse all the way. I'd get back to Newport if I were you!' Tryon said, 'Captain, please take the wheel for a minute,' and winked to me to go below with him. Out of the Captain's hearing he said: 'I wish very much to get home and I think we can make it all right. Mix the Captain a glass of grog and make it stiff. I'll send him down to get it and we will observe the effect.' The Captain disposed of the drink, came again on deck, and now, as he gazed at the stormy scene, the scowl faded away and he exclaimed, 'Tryon, this is all right! Let her go for Padanaram!' So we kept on and in due time made port, though much storm-beaten and well wet-down.

Tryon's personality had a curious attraction for strangers. He was always making chance acquaintances and having amusing little adventures with people. One summer, when lying in Newport Harbor in his boat, we went ashore for a ramble in the outskirts of the town, taking our sketch-boxes. Tryon went to a moorland north of Bailey's Beach, I to the beach itself. We agreed to meet at the wharf in the evening. Tryon was dressed in a blue flannel shirt, a well-worn pair of corduroy knickerbockers, rough woolen stockings and hobnailed shoes. He wore a faded yachting cap, with a glazed visor. His heavy pack was slung on his back, he was bronzed and swarthy, and in his outward appearance he did not seem to fit, exactly, into the picture ashore — the ultra-fashionable atmosphere of Bellevue Avenue and the Casino. At evening I reached the wharf first and was waiting for him. It was long before the gasoline era. Presently a victoria, one of Newport's most dashing and elegant equipages, drove down upon the wharf. A coachman and footman in white doeskin breeches and patent-leather boots sat behind a span of chestnut thoroughbreds with docked tails, who champed their snaffle bits rattling their silver chains. As the carriage drew nearer, I saw in it a handsome woman in a filmy white gown, carrying a gay parasol trimmed with lace; and beside her sat Tryon, in his rough garb, his dusty shoes, and with his sketching impedimenta piled at their feet, a striking foil to her aristocratic elegance. He alighted, raised his cap and thanked her, and she drove away. I said, 'You seem to be adapting yourself quickly to our surroundings.' He smiled and replied, 'She picked me up as I trudged along the road. It was hot and dusty and I surely appreciated it. And,' he added, 'we had a very interesting conversation.'

When Tryon settled in South Dartmouth in 1883, he invited the pupils of his New York classes to join him in the country, saying he would be glad to criticize their sketches without pay, with the understanding that he should give this help irregularly, at his own convenience. He insisted upon complete freedom for himself in summer to fish, cruise, or loaf at will. So it happened that a group of his pupils gathered about him, for a time, at Padanaram, and the memories of those days are Arcadian indeed.

Tryon usually criticized the work of the sketch class about once a week, devoting a morning to it, but except for that he and I spent our days, in July and August, upon the water. We started out soon after breakfast with the first puffs of the summer breeze and returned only with the dropping of the wind, about four or five o'clock. After supper, Tryon and his pupils, men and women, gathered in a disused barn belonging to Judith Howland, who kept the comfortable boarding-house in which the students lived. Its wide doorway opened pleasantly upon the street. There were hammocks and a swing, and here in the summer evenings we held symposiums upon many and varied themes.

Tryon usually laid up his boat early in October. By that time the summer residents and most of the art students had departed. With the coming of frost and the rich colors of autumn he turned his attention to the country and began to sketch and paint. Sometimes he painted a complete picture, of good size, directly from nature, at two or three sittings, if the weather and effect remained the same. Then again he would make a quick sketch of some transient theme of the moment, moving clouds and fitful sunshine, over the autumn fields. We explored the old pastures and woodlands of many an abandoned farm, we sketched in the haze of Indian summer, or, on brisk cool autumn days, ate our lunch together lying in the sun, sheltered from the wind by a stone wall. Allen Howe, a pupil of Tryon's, sometimes prolonged his stay into the fall, and we often met at Tryon's house after supper and spent the long autumn evening before a roaring wood fire. We scraped down antique furniture, the spoil of country auctions, ate apples and walnuts, popped corn, and drank cider or the spicy hot rum punch which Tryon brewed and in which he took justifiable pride. He greatly enjoyed a fire on the hearth and built one upon the slightest pretext. To save chopping wood he had the unique habit of entering the living-room with as long a log or fence rail as the space permitted, and, thrusting one end of it into the fireplace, he fed it to the flames as fast as they consumed it. This entertaining performance disturbed the household not a little, as it scattered dust and cinders about. Then, too, when he forgot to tend his log, the fire crept out along it into the room and threatened your clothing, the rugs, and the house itself. One windy night, as we were leaving, after an evening spent before one of these open fires, we were startled to see a rain of sparks and burning coals pouring upon the roof from the chimney like a display of fireworks. Tryon had out-

201

done himself with fence rails, old lobster pot buoys, and drift-wood, and when we called his attention to the result, he thought it prudent to go in and put water on the blaze.

After long experience I learned that when Tryon summoned me to go fishing I might as well drop everything and join him. His invitation was brief and to the point. 'Bring your old clothes, but no tackle, for I have plenty. And plan to stay awhile.' He sent out few false alarms. If ever the fish failed him after my arrival, he was apologetic but philosophic, for, as he said, if fishing were a dead sure thing, it would lose its in-terest. He would, however, mildly berate the recalcitrant fish.

Long before sunrise, when the first faint light of an August morning dimly entered my room in Tryon's cottage at South Dartmouth, I have awakened to find him standing by the bed. He had stolen quietly in not to disturb the other members of the household. With a cheerful smile he whispered, 'Want to go fishing?' I dressed hastily and we snatched a cup of coffee and a piece of bread in the kitchen. What a morning! Outside, the still air was fragrant with salt odors of rockweed and kelp, at low tide. The grass dripped with the heavy dew. A heron rose and flapped away with a shrill screech. We rowed off to the channel opposite Tryon's house. Silently laying the oars in the boat, Tryon anchored without a splash, for any undue noise might have endangered our chances.

The glow in the eastern sky over the sleeping village in-creased and a few clouds low on the horizon were edged with rose. Night mists still lingered over the water. The sun would soon be up. 'People often ask me,' said Tryon, 'when and where I see the effects I paint, the dawn, the evening, the moonlight. I tell them I see many motives for future pictures

202

when I am fishing. I am up by four o'clock on most mornings in summer and enjoy the moods of Nature denied to those who sleep late. I would not miss this lovely hour for anything, in fact I feel that all time spent in bed in summer is wasted and I begrudge it.' So we fished out the tide and with a dozen or twenty magnificent squitteague, weighing all told forty or fifty pounds, we rowed home to enjoy a hearty breakfast at eight o'clock.

For a good many years, Tryon had cast longing glances at southern waters as a new and inviting field for his fishing. He devoured all the literature that dealt with his favorite sport, and his imagination, aided by the glowing accounts given by fishermen of the South, pictured to him new and novel experiences. As he grew older and his winter's work, combined with the cold, became more irksome, he dreamed of basking in the sunshine under Southern skies and trying his skill upon the tarpon, the amberjack, the spotted sea-trout, and studying the brilliantly colored fish and marine life of the tropics. 'Some day,' he used to say to me, 'we must pack up and go South, dodge a Northern winter and try the fishing. It probably will be a disappointment, as I have usually found the much-advertised fishing resorts to be; but we will, at least, see a new country, and I long for the warmth, as I dread the winter here more and more. Furthermore, we shall have a glorious time in anticipating and planning for it; and what an orgy of purchasing new tackle we can indulge in. I am not at all particular how I go, but on general principles I like the water rather than the cars. In the interim, we can both "inquire" as Whistler advised the critics to do....'

Accordingly, after spending months in studying maps, writing letters to Southern fishing resorts in Florida and elsewhere, late in the winter of 1909 we took ship in a coast-line steamer for Jacksonville. Thence we traveled across the State to Fort Myers, on the Caloosahatchie River, then to Punta Rassa on the Gulf of Mexico. It was Tryon's first experience of the South and the effect of the country and its inhabitants upon his active, energetic nature, as dynamic as an electric battery, was amusing. The laziness, the happy-go-lucky procrastinating Southern manner of life, first bewildered Tryon, then irritated him. But eventually he took it good-humoredly and made the best of it, and we found entertainment in it, especially with the darkies.

Alas! for the rosy dreams of fishermen who never are, but always to be, blest. We soon found that the Southern fish had a close kinship with the human species of the locality. One morning's fishing aroused our suspicions, the second confirmed them. 'Why,' said Tryon, 'these fish are just like the people here! They have no pep!' After a week of it our interest evaporated, and we spent the remainder of our time either on a schooner yacht belonging to one of Tryon's friends, a retired admiral of the Navy whom we found cruising in the Gulf of Mexico, or explored a little of the country about Punta Rassa. One day I decided to make a final trial of the fishing. Tryon said he had had enough and would take a trip to Sanibel Island on the little excursion steamer for the day. He returned with his luncheon knapsack crammed with rare seashells. Neither of us had known that the sea beach of this island is world famous for the variety and beauty of its shells. Tryon described them as piled in windrows. He regretted he could carry away so few.

The landscape of Florida we both found extremely uninteresting and depressing, and the climate debilitating. We returned North in March with a renewed appreciation of the congenial latitude of the forties, in spite, or because, of its rigors. At all events, we had enjoyed the experience. Though we caught a good many fish, we neither saw nor hooked any tarpon, as we were a month or more too early for them.

Tryon always spoke with pleasure of his acquaintance with Grover Cleveland when the latter was President, and when they, together with Joseph Jefferson, often fished together for striped bass at the head of Buzzard's Bay, near Gray Gables, Cleveland's summer home. The three of them often lay on the bank of the tidal river, in the shade of an old fish house, and told stories while waiting for the tide to make. Tryon described Cleveland as a man of few words, though not unsociable. He said he was very simple in his manner and very democratic, and that, while he did not often speak, when he did it was much to the point; and that he would join in the laughter at a good story as if he enjoyed it. Tryon said that Cleveland was a genuine fisherman. He loved to fish whether he caught anything or not, and would go off in a rowboat by himself and fish alone for hours at a time. He had a small catboat called the Ruth which he used a great deal, but he did not like motor-boats. Tryon enjoyed the local anecdotes of Cleveland, whose rough appearance when he was fishing often misled people. Tryon related that one day Cleveland, anchored in a rowboat, was having excellent luck with the tautog. Seeing him pulling in the fish, a party of would-be anglers came alongside and asked him to act as their guide, offering to pay him well. Cleveland was not responsive, and, thinking they had not made the induce-

205

ment sufficient, the fishermen said, 'Well, what wages did you earn last year?' 'Fifty thousand dollars,' replied Cleveland.

At Ogunquit on the coast of Maine, Tryon found ideal conditions for a month's sojourn in the fall, both to fish and to sketch. A small tidal river here finds the sea and separates a succession of bold rocky headlands from one of the finest beaches of our eastern seaboard. Three miles of hard golden brown and white sand lie to the ocean at so slight an angle that the surf breaks far off shore and throws long sweeps and secondary rollers up the gentle slope. This beach and its supporting sand dunes separate the lower reaches of the Ogunquit River from the sea for the distance of a mile or two, and, in calm or storm, it is the setting for an ever-changing marine panorama of grandeur and beauty. Tryon often said it was the finest bit of seacoast he knew. And, to perfect it for him, there was good fishing.

He always referred to his sojourns at Ogunquit with the greatest pleasure. He began to go there in 1907, for a few weeks in September, and returned for several succeeding years. Soon after his arrival on his first visit I received an enthusiastic letter from him describing the charms of the place, its subjects for painting and its fishing. The boarding-house, too, was much to his taste, and when he invited me to join him he warned me, as usual, to take nothing but old clothes, for, as he wrote, 'It isn't dressy here.' Which was a superfluous admonition, for I knew if it had been he wouldn't have been there.

The cottage in which we had rooms stood on a bluff above the river. The ocean was just beyond and the roar of the surf was never stilled. Our windows looked to the east and we could see the sun and the moon rise over the sea. The air of Maine in the early fall, especially at the seashore, is like a draught of wine. Crisp mornings and evenings, warm noons, the fragrance of the pines and the sea, a scent of wood smoke in the air, goldenrod and blue asters, late marigolds and dahlias in the dooryards — don't go there, reader, unless you are able to return, for you will be homesick for it when the year rolls round. Tryon and I fished there for the young pollack on each flood tide. Then, when the fish were not rising, we enjoyed the magnificent beach or took walks along the cliffs.

On quiet afternoons as we lay, comfortably propped up in holes dug in the beach sand, watching the long rollers lazily breaking off shore, sending in wavelets at our feet, Tryon, filled with the peaceful charm of the hour, quoted 'The Lotus Eaters':

> 'In the afternoon they came unto a land
> In which it seemed always afternoon.
> All round the coast the languid air did swoon
> Breathing like one that hath a weary dream.'

Again, when the storm broke, he strode along the cliffs, leaning hard against the wind, and shouted, above the thunder of the surf, to me to join him, to see the spouting of the sea in geysers high into the air through a blow-hole in the rocks. He was deeply moved and thrilled with it all. And he often told me he considered Ogunquit to be perhaps the most grandly typical spot of the whole coast of Maine.

The spirit of the sea, the surf breaking on the rocks and beach in calm and storm, the endless variety of wave forms, of water in motion, fascinated and held Tryon to the exclusion of the other more obvious aspects of Ogunquit. There was, however, a rugged region back of the village which he some-

207

times explored, jotting down a hasty note of its anatomy in pencil. But he spent most of his time on or near the sea, as was his habit everywhere.

He loved to explore new localities and taste their indigenous flavors. Every detail interested him. There was a little grotto among the rocks of the shore a mile or two south of Ogunquit, called the 'Devil's Kitchen,' accessible only at low tide. In it were rock pools full of sea anemones and limpets, and when the tide was out, it reeked with odors of kelp and rockweed. We liked to gloat over its treasures with the zest of children first viewing Nature's wonders. Together we crawled into this cavern and listened to the sonorous echoes of our voices, compressed and intensified by the low ceiling and confined space; and, from its dark recesses, viewed the little picture of blue sea and sunlit sky seen through the jagged entrance.

A small beach adjoined this cave, covered thickly with gray pebbles. They were worn smooth as satin by the sea's incessant polishing; and their stratification with a darker stone painted innumerable little landscapes upon them. They fascinated Tryon, who was as quick to see suggestions of beauty in natural objects as Leonardo to discover hints of designs in the stains on old walls and in the veinings of marble; so we often lay outstretched upon this stony beach and selected symphonies in blue, gray, and black on the little ovals like the ink painting of Sesshu, the silhouette of a dwarfed pine or cedar, a little moonlight, or a misty mountain range. Absorbed by their unlimited variety and suggestiveness, we stuffed our pockets with these pebbles until they would hold no more. Then, as we staggered homeward under the load, we began to throw away the less interesting pieces, until our trips to the Devil's Kitchen could be traced by the continuous trail of discarded pebbles along the path.

Until he was seventy-four years old, Tryon showed scarcely a trace of advancing age. When he sailed and fished, he handled his boat alone as easily as ever. Two years before he died we were trolling for mackerel one day in the Skat near Dumpling Light, about three miles from South Dartmouth. As we stood back and forth over the fish and among the flying gulls, Tryon sighted a dark object in the water about the size of a bushel basket, just under the surface, over which hundreds of gulls screamed and dove. It was a 'pod' or solid mass of small bait fish driven together by the voracious mackerel, who rushed at and fed upon them from below while the gulls attacked them from above. I was sailing the boat and Tryon had stopped fishing, but, always alert and curious of the least of Nature's signs, when he saw this pod of bait fish he said quickly, 'Let me take her!' Seizing a dip net, he maneuvered the sailboat nearer and nearer the dark object, tiller in one hand, net in the other. Finally he put the Skat over the pod and, making a quick scoop, got a handful of the small fish. 'I wanted to see what the mackerel were feeding on,' he said. 'To-morrow I will use these silversides for bait.'

Often, as we sailed or fished, a philosophic or retrospective mood would steal upon him. It was on the afternoon I have just mentioned that we sailed past the summer residence of a millionaire on the Nonquitt shore, a great stone structure, with grounds elaborately laid out, long wharves projecting into the bay, motor-boats and all the appurtenances of such places. Among other developments the owner had built a massive sea-wall which the winter storms had handled rather roughly, crumbling it away and eating into the land. Tryon and I had known the place in our younger days when it was virgin soil and we had loved its natural aspect. I said, 'What a pity to destroy the beauty of that spot and to deprive it of Nature's own protection, the rocks and the beach which for years kept it intact.' 'Yes,' said Tryon, 'the one secret of happiness which seems denied to most people is that of simplicity of life. That man's money is a curse to him, for it makes him restless and he seeks diversion for his mind in the accumulation of more and ever more material possessions. The capacity to enjoy Nature as she is and simple things is true wealth. I could well afford to have a schooner yacht with captain and crew, I have been tempted sometimes to own a larger boat, but I have always resisted it, and here I am, at the end of my days, with the same equipment with which I started in youth.'

XVI

LAST DAYS

From sixty to seventy Tryon painted fewer pictures. Acknowledging his debt to Time, he preferred to maintain a high standard of quality, though he might do but little work. Accordingly he reduced the size and restricted the number of his paintings. But, to the very end, there was no sign of weakness or falling off in the conception or execution of them. The last landscapes that he painted are among his most successful achievements, as varied in theme, as beautiful in form and color, and as masterly in their technique as any he ever did.

As late as the summer of 1924, I could not discover any diminution of his physical strength or his activity in his life out-of-doors in summer. We were sailing up the harbor of Padanaram one day in his catboat when Tryon was well over seventy. On one side of us was Walton Ricketson, then past eighty, alone in a fast sailing boat, and on the other side was another veteran, a contemporary of Tryon's, in still another smart craft. We had an informal race on the way home. I said, 'These old boys, along with you, will probably be sailing boats at the age of a hundred — long after I have passed on.' Tryon looked thoughtful for a moment, glanced at the old men in the other boats, then turned to me, smiled faintly, and said, 'We don't know.'

It was, I think, about two years before his death that we were sitting together at dinner in South Dartmouth one evening, when he suddenly rose from the table, excused himself, and went into the next room. He returned in a few moments and said: 'I have been troubled for some time past with a convulsive contraction of my throat when I try to swallow. It soon passes, but it is disagreeable while it lasts.' It was the first symptom of the disease, cancer of the stomach, which slowly developed and from which he died.

Early in the winter of 1924, it was evident that Tryon was seriously ill and that his strength was failing rapidly. He could still go about, though he kept much at home. In mid-winter he stopped painting, never to resume it. Though he was as cheerful as ever, and spoke hopefully about his health, as if he expected to regain it, I am certain that he knew he had not long to live. He faced death with the greatest courage and with philosophical composure. As the spring of 1925 drew on and the time came for him to go to the country, he looked forward eagerly to it, hoping that the change would benefit him. I went frequently to see him, and was able to help him transact a few matters of business preparatory to his departure. As we were talking of these one day, not long before he left, he spoke of his condition, and said to me: 'I do not fear death. It is a perfectly natural event, and a part of life. I have no regrets, and I cannot complain. I feel that I have been unusually blessed and most fortunate in my life. I have had perfect health for over seventy years and I have been able to do the work I loved. I have lived

212

fully and happily. I have enjoyed life. I hoped that I was to have a little more of it, but it is not to be.' It was difficult for me to reply, for, while it evidently gave him satisfaction to say what he did, I knew he neither wished for nor expected perfunctory words of sympathy. But to make as fitting a response as I could, I spoke briefly of thoughts that had sustained us both during the long years of our friendship. 'If,' said Socrates, just before his death, 'the night one sleeps the soundest is a sweet experience, what is the difference to us between a few hours and ten thousand years?' — 'It is pleasant to die if there be gods, sad to live if there be none.' To which he answered simply that he thought, as we had often said to each other, that this was true faith.

On April 22, I escorted Tryon and his family to the Fall River steamboat, his usual means of getting to South Dartmouth. We all felt that he was leaving New York never to return. On June 3, I visited him in South Dartmouth and found that he had failed very much. On June 17, I went to see him again and for the last time. He sat up at intervals, but lay most of the time on a couch in his living-room. He had been unable to take food or nourishment for weeks, but he was still cheerful. He said to me, 'They say you can't live without food or sleep, but I have disproved it.' As he lay on the couch he held in his hands a Japanese plate of carved tortoise-shell, extremely delicate in its intricate and beautiful design. He turned it about and caressed it, and said to me, 'After all, beauty is the one lasting and immortal thing.'

On July 1, 1925, Tryon died. His mind had been unclouded until the end, in spite of severe suffering during the last months of his life. In one of the last moments he said, with a motion of

213

his hands, 'The line should be about so long,' as though referring to fishing.

He is buried on a site selected by himself, a hillside facing
the west, overlooking the harbor of South Dartmouth, in a
cemetery about a mile distant from his house. A granite boulder
marks his grave.

In the fifty years during which Tryon's art steadily advanced
until he was an acknowledged master, many changes have
taken place in this country, not a few in the world of art. It
seemed, to many, that the little group of philosophers and poets
who made Concord a literary shrine in the mid-century might
be the precursors of a school of thought and of great achievements in literature. So it seemed to some of us that the group
of our artists who, in the seventies and eighties, brought home
the fine traditions of French art and its science, and carried
them on so successfully, might open the way for worthy suc-
cessors.

But, as Lewis Mumford has so plainly demonstrated
of Emerson, Thoreau, and Whitman, of Hawthorne and
man Melville, was our Golden Day in Literature
incident. And, by inference, and from our observation
aberrant laws, if laws they are, that govern the
disappearance of periods of artistic activity and accomplishment, it would seem safe to predict that considerable time will
elapse before America again produces artists of the stature of
Thayer and La Farge, of Whistler, Dewing, and Tryon, of
Wyant, Inness, and Martin, of Ryder and Homer. Rodin,
commenting on our art of the seventies and eighties, said,
'America has had a Renaissance, but America doesn't know it.'

But, while we do not know what the future holds, we

say, with Whistler, 'We have then but to wait — until, with the mark of the gods upon him, there come among us again the chosen, who shall continue what has gone before. Satisfied that, even were he never to appear, the story of the beautiful is already complete....' So we may, for the present, rest content, thankful for what is already a rich heritage of beauty left us by these men.

FINIS

APPENDIX

MEDALS AND AWARDS

Associate of the National Academy in 1890; Academician in 1891.

Member of the Society of American Artists, 1882; American Water Color Society; National Institute of Arts and Letters.

Awarded bronze medal at Boston, 1882; Gold medals, American Art Association, 1886 and 1887; Third Hallgarten prize, National Academy of Design, 1887; Ellsworth prize, Art Institute of Chicago, 1888; Palmer prize, Chicago Interstate Exposition, 1889; Webb prize, Society of American Artists, 1889; First-Class gold medal, Munich Exposition, 1892; Medal, Columbian Exposition, Chicago, 1893; First prize, Cleveland Interstate Exposition, 1895; First prize, Tennessee Centennial, Nashville, 1897; Gold medal ($1500), 1898, and Chronological medal, 1899, Carnegie Institute, Pittsburgh; Gold medal, Pan-American Exposition, Buffalo, 1901; Gold medal, St. Louis Exposition, 1904; Silver medal, Panama-Pacific Exposition, San Francisco, 1915.

Tryon is represented by works in the following public galleries: Freer Gallery, Washington, D.C.; Corcoran Gallery, Washington, D.C.; National Gallery of Art, Washington, D.C.; Metropolitan Museum of Art, New York City; Toledo Museum of Art; Worcester Museum; Pennsylvania Academy of the Fine Arts, Philadelphia; Herron Art Institute, Indianapolis; Detroit Institute of Arts; Montclair, New Jersey, Art Museum; Hackley Art Gallery, Muskegon, Michigan; Rhode Island School of Design, Providence, Rhode Island; Butler Art Institute, Youngstown, Ohio; Wadsworth Atheneum, Hartford, Connecticut; Tryon Art Gallery, Smith College, Northampton, Massachusetts.

217

BIBLIOGRAPHY

Tryon, Dwight W.: *Charles François Daubigny — Modern French Masters*. Edited by J. C. Vandyke. The Century Company, New York, 1896.

Tryon, Dwight W.: List of pictures by the artist since 1909, with the names of their owners. To supplement list in Caffin's *Art of Dwight W. Tryon*, three-page typed copy in Forbes Library, Northampton.

Caffin, Charles H.: *American Masters of Painting*. Doubleday, Page and Company, New York, 1902, pp. 155–67.

Caffin, Charles H.: *The Art of Dwight W. Tryon — An Appreciation*. (Monograph.) The Forest Press, New York, 1919.

Churchill, Alfred V.: 'Dwight W. Tryon, M.A., N.A.,' *Bulletin* of Smith College, Hillyer Art Gallery, March 30, 1924.

Churchill, Alfred V.: 'Tryon at Smith College — 1886–1923.' *Smith College Alumnæ Quarterly*, November, 1925.

Cortissoz, Royal: 'Some Imaginative Types in American Art,' *Harper's Magazine*, vol. 91, July, 1895, p. 171.

French, H. W.: *Art and Artists in Connecticut*. Lee and Shepard, Boston, 1879.

Hartman, Sadakichi: *A History of American Art*. L. C. Page and Company, Boston, 1902, vol. 1, pp. 127–36.

Isham, Samuel: *History of American Painting*. The Macmillan Company, 1915, pp. 454–57, 476–83.

Merrick, Lula: 'Tryon, Devotee of Nature,' *International Studio*, September, 1923, vol. 77, pp. 498–504.

Phillips, Duncan: 'Dwight Tryon,' *American Magazine of Art*, August, 1918, vol. 9, pp. 391–92.

Sherman, Frederic F.: 'Dwight W. Tryon,' *American Painters of Yesterday and Today*. New York. Privately printed, 1919.

Sherman, Frederic F.: 'Landscapes by Tryon,' *Art in America*, December, 1918, vol. 7, pp. 31–38.

White, Henry C.: 'D. W. Tryon — An Appreciation.' *Bulletin* of Smith College, Hillyer Art Gallery, March 30, 1924.

Appleton's Cyclopædia of American Biography, vol. 6, p. 171.
Century Cyclopædia of Names.
Encyclopædia Britannica, 'Dwight William Tryon.' Fourteenth edition, vol. 22, p. 524.
International Studio: 'Work of Tryon.' March, 1900, vol. 10, Supplement, pp. 3–4.
National Encyclopædia of American Biography, vol. 8, p. 423.
Nelson's Looseleaf Encyclopædia, vol. 12, p. 200.

INDEX

INDEX

Abbey, Edwin Austin, 159
Ackerman, Frederick, architect, 108
Albright Gallery in Buffalo, 89
Alice, cruising sloop, 194
American Renaissance, 214
Apponagansett Harbor, 2
Arnold, Matthew, quoted, 73
Art Students' League, 91
Artist, two qualities of, 148
Artists, New England attitude toward, in 1873, 28, 29
Avery, Samuel P., collector, 24

Baker, Capt. 'Arch,' 196
Barbizon School, 36
Barker, Oliver, driver of stage-coach, 193
Batterson, James G., his paintings, 20
Belden, Alice H., marries Tryon, 24; death, 24
Belden, Celestia, 24
Belden, Seabury, 24
Belknap, Leverett, quoted on Tryon, 17, 23
Bell, Arthur H., artist, 47
Bell, Edward A., artist, 120, 137, 146, 155
Bellini, Giovanni, altarpiece of, 49, 50
Bennett, Dr. T. L., 158
Bickmore, Prof., of the Museum of Natural History, 118, 147
Bixby, W. K., connoisseur, 147
Blakelock, artist, 90, 120, 140
Block Island, 30–32
Bode, Dr., of the Berlin Museum, 79
Bonnat, Léon Joseph Florentin, 159

Boston Public Library, mural decorations in, 159
Brandegee, Robert, artist, 43, 90
Brown and Gross, booksellers, 16
Browning, Robert, quoted, 63, 122
Brush, George DeForest, 36, 81, 90, 171
Burton, Rev. Dr. Nathaniel J., 27
Bushnell, Dr. Horace, 27–29
Bushnell, Mary, 29

Caffin, Charles H., critic, quoted, 37, 162, 163–65, 172
Cancale, Brittany, 48
Canvas, for painting, 175, 176
Carnegie Art Institute, 158; exhibition of 1898, 162
Cazin, paintings of, 7
Champney, J. Wells, teacher of drawing at Smith College, 89
Channing, William Ellery, 193
Chase, William M., 36
Chavannes, Puvis de, his mural decorations, 159
Cheney, Col. Frank, 29
Chicago Art Institute, 78
Church, Frederick E., artist, 19
Churchill, Alfred V., on Tryon, 99, 103, 105, 118, 181
Clarke, Thomas B., collector, 76
Clemens, Samuel L., 27, 28
Cleveland, Grover, 117, 205
Cole, Thomas, view of Mount Etna by, 19
Colt's Firearms Factory, Hartford, 15

223

Connecticut River Valley, 10
Constable, John, 154
Corot, Jean Baptiste Camille, 56; anecdote of, 69
Cortissoz, Royal, quoted on Tryon, 151, 155, 160, 173
Courbet, Gustave, 40, 41
Cox, Kenyon, 36

Dana, R. H., his 'Two Years Before the Mast,' 60
Darley, F. O. C., copy of engraving by, 18
Daubigny, Charles, his influence on Tryon, 35, 44, 45, 49
Decamp, Joseph, 36
Defoe, Daniel, 122
Dewing, Thomas W., artist, 36, 74, 75, 80, 81, 120, 124, 170; his decorations in Freer's house, 81; his view of Millet's peasants, 85; his 'A Flute-Player,' 90; his canoeing adventure, 133–35; his friendship with Tryon, 139–41; Cortissoz on, 151, 152, 154
Dewing, Mrs. Thomas W., 110, 141
Donald, Rev. J. A., letter of, 125, 147
Dordrecht, Holland, 48
Drawing of the antique, Jacquesson's principles, 41–43
Dufferin, Lord, his 'Letters from High Latitudes,' 123
Duveneck, Frank, 36

East Chester, 58
East Hartford, Conn., 8–14
Edwards, George Wharton, artist, 74, 139
Emerson, Ralph Waldo, 72, 122, 165; on mysticism, 148
'Eve Repentant,' statue of, 20
Eyre, Wilson, Freer's house designed by, 81

Faxon, William Bailey, artist, 74, 139; Tryon's first sale made to, 22
Fedden, Romilly, artist, his book, 'Golden Days,' 123
Fenger, his 'Alone in the Caribbean,' 135
Fitch, Raymond, brother-in-law of Tryon, 136
Fitz, Benjamin R., artist, 145
Flagg, Charles, at Jacquesson's school, 43
Flagg, Montague, at Jacquesson's school, 43

Florida, 204, 205
Freer, Charles L., and Tryon, 76–87; his Detroit house, 81–84, 160, 161
Freer Gallery, 77, 78, 81, 158, 167, 168

Gifford, R. Swain, landscape painter, 58, 74, 137, 139
Granville, Normandy, 48
Guernsey, a visit to, 47
Guillemet, J. B. A., his influence on Tryon, 45, 46

Hamerton, P. G., quoted on the landscape painter, 13; his biography of Turner, 52, 54
Hannum's Business School, Hartford, 17
Hardy, Thomas, 59
Harpignies, 35, 44
Harris, Victor, composer, 117, 147
Hartford, Conn., 8, 10, 12, 15–25; the studio at, 26–33; conditions of life in, in 1873, 26, 27
Hassam, artist, 81, 90
Hayricks, 61
Hecker, Col. Frank J., 77
Hermit, a, 67
Herreshoff, Nat, 133
Hillyer, Mrs., 29
Hillyer Art Galleries, 107
Hockanum, 9
Homer, Winslow, 81
Howe, Allen, 201
Howland, Judith, 200
Howland, Capt. William Henry, 196–98
Hudson River School, 24
Hunt, William Morris, 36, 89, 96, 102

Ibsen, Henrik, 165
Imagination, true creative and mystical, 148
Impressionism, 149
Impressionists, 36
Ingres, Jean Auguste Dominique, 35, 38–40, 92
Inness, George, artist, 36, 76, 80, 152
International Exposition, Munich, 1892, 78

Jefferson, Joseph, 74, 117, 205

Kingsley, Eldridge, 83, 161
Knowlton, Helen M., 96

La Chevreuse, Jacquesson de ('Jackson's'), his school, 35, 37, 38, 41, 42, 92
La Farge, John, artist, 36, 75, 95, 182
Landscape painter, environment of, 13
La Rochefoucauld, François de, 72
Latour, Fantin, letter of Whistler to, 39
Lawrence, Sir Thomas, portrait of West by, 19
Lepage, Bastien, his portrait of his father, 51
Loggia dei Lanzi, statues of the, 20
Low, Will H., artist, 36, 74, 139
Lucas, E. V., quoted, 154

Maine, the air of, in early fall, 206, 207
Mansfield, Burton, painting of Tryon in collection of, 66
Marines, 167–69, 173
Marquand, Henry G., portrait of, 171
Martin, Homer, 76
Melville, Herman, his 'Moby Dick,' 60; his association with New Bedford, 193
Metcalf, artist, 81
Millet, Jean François, a saying of, 165; anecdote of, 182
Mills, beloved by painters, 11
Modernistic painting, 171
Montross, N. E., 75, 139, 160, **172**
Montross Art Galleries, 75
Moore, George, 59
Mumford, Lewis, 214
Mural decoration, a cardinal principle of, 159
Murphy, J. Francis, painter, 75
Mysticism, 148

Naubuc, 10
New Bedford, Mass., 1, 59–61; literary and artistic associations of, 193
New Bedford Yacht Club, 4, 72
Niemeyer, J. H., teacher of drawing at Smith College, and later professor at the Yale School of Fine Arts, 89
Nonquitt, 58

Ogunquit, Maine, 66, 84, 116, 149, 167, 206–09
Ogunquit River, 124, 206
Omakitsu, painting by, 168

Painting, on wood panels, 175, 177; on canvas, 175, 176; on mahogany and whitewood panels, 176; ground, 177; pastel paper, 178; fixatives, 178–80
Palmer, Potter, 77, 78
'Pandanaram.' See South Dartmouth
Panels, wood, for painting, 175, 177; mahogany and whitewood, 176
Parker, Rev. Dr. Edwin P., 27
Pastel, 166, 167
'Peacock Room,' 80, 81
Post, Miss, pupil of Tryon, 96–98
Proctor, Phimister, 75

Quamquisset, 195

Raeburn, Sir Henry, portrait by, 19
Rhode Island School of Design at Providence, picture of Tryon at, 65
Richards, W. T., 24
Ricketson, Daniel, 193
Ricketson, Walter, 211
Roberts, Martha, aunt of Dwight, 8
Roberts family, 8, 9
Robinson, Edwin Arlington, sonnet of, 29
Rodin, Auguste, quoted, 214
Rogers, William A., of Buffalo, 158
Rossiter, E. K., architect, 118, 146, 147
Ryder, Albert, P., artist, 75, 90, 188, 193

Salt-making, 61
Sanibel Island, seashells of, 204
Sargent, John Singer, 159, 171
Sark, 47, 48
Sartain, William, artist, 74, 139
Schilling, Alexander, artist, 75
Seelye, Pres. L. Clark, of Smith College, 88–90; letter from, 107
Shakespeare, William, 122
Shirlaw, Walter, 36
Skat, the catboat, 4, 5, 136
Skinner, Otis, and Tryon, 23; at Jacquesson's school, 43
Smith, Virginia J., her appreciation of Tryon, 99
Smith College, works of Tryon at, 48, 49, 63, 170; the study of art at, 88, 89; art collection at, 90; art gallery presented to, by Tryon, 108, 109
Society of American Artists, 36
South Dartmouth, Mass., 2, 4, 58–73, 193, 195

225

Steel engraving, 52
Stowe, Prof. Calvin E., 27
Stowe, Harriet Beecher, 27
Strong, Beulah, letter to, quoted, 63; assistant of Tryon in Smith College Art School, 98

Tarbell, Edmund C., artist, 90
Tennyson, Alfred, 'The Lotus Eaters,' 207
Thayer, Abbott H., artist, 36, 80, 81; his friendship with Tryon, 47, 141, 142; his 'Angels,' 90; his theories of art, 142–45; as creative artist, 170, 171
Thoreau, Henry David, 72, 122, 193; a saying of, 150
Thornbury, George Walter, his life of Turner, 52, 54, 130
Traveling, 50
Tryon, Anson, father of Dwight, 7, 8
Tryon, Delia O. Roberts, mother of Dwight, 7, 8; secures position as custodian of pictures in Wadsworth Athenæum, 19, 20
Tryon, Dwight William, the approach to, 1–6; his cottage at South Dartmouth, Mass., 2, 3, 58; his summer studio, 3, 4; birth, 7; parents and ancestors, 7–9; his boyhood at East Hartford, 8–14; his early drawing and painting, 10, 11, 12; his fondness for the water, 11, 13, 32, 33; his love of Nature, 12, 32; removes to Hartford, 14; his luck, 15; works in Firearms Factory, 15; works in bookstore, 16, 21; his personality, 17; becomes expert in writing, 18; his pen-and-ink drawings, 18; early sources of his inspiration, 19–21; his reading, 21, 22, 23; makes his first sale, 22; hesitates between art and medicine as a profession, 22, 23, 25; exhibits at National Academy of Design, 24; marriage, 24; chooses art as profession, 25–29; his Hartford studio, 29–33; gives instruction in drawing and painting, 29; visits Mount Desert, White Mountains, and Block Island, 30; in Paris, 34–46; his mastery of form, 39; foreign influences upon, 44–57; sketching trips of, 47–49; effect of European experience upon, 48, 49; letters of, 49–51; at East Chester, 58; his life at South Dartmouth, 58–73; his earlier and later style of painting compared, 62, 74, 76; his literary interest, 72; his New York studio, 74; turns to teaching, 74, 88, 89; exhibits at Montross Galleries, 75, 139; his friendship with Freer, 76–87; decorated room in Freer's Detroit house, 81–84, 160, 161; becomes Professor of Art at Smith College, 89; his views on art teaching, 91; his advice on taking up art as a profession, 91; his class in drawing and painting, 92, 93, 96, 97; his teaching, 94–96, 99–106, 185; his theory of instruction in Smith, 98; resigns from Smith, 107; receives degree of Master of Arts from Smith, 107; presents art gallery to Smith, 108, 109; word-picture of, 110–13; his garden, 113, 114; his clothes, 114, 115; his social habits, 116, 117; his range of human contacts, 117, 118; his sense of humor, 119; his winter abodes, 119–21; his reading, 122, 123; his fondness for music, 123; of complex nature, 123; his fortune and use of money, 124; his generosity, 125; his temperament, 126–28; his love of children, 129; his reverence, 129; his diversion of fishing and sailing, 129–38; his friends, 139–47; his critical faculty, 146; his art, 148–58; his decorative work, 158–63; a summary of his qualities as painter, 164, 165; his work in pastel, 166, 167; marines of, 167–69, 173; figure paintings of, 169, 170; self-portraits of, 170; watercolors of, 170; etchings, 170; development of his art, 171; his comments on art, 172, 173; charm of his pictures, 173, 174; materials used by, 176–80; his methods, 180–83; his financial success, 184–90; regarded his art in unworldly way, 188–90; recollections of, 191, 192, 201; cruising in his first sloop, 194–99; his acquaintance with captains of South Dartmouth, 195, 196; anecdote of, 199; invites pupils to South Dartmouth, 200; on fishing trips, 202–05, 209; his first southern trip, 204; and Cleveland, 205; at Ogunquit, 206–09; in a philosophic mood, 209, 210; his later years, 211; last illness, 212, 213; death, 213; burial place, 214; medals and awards, 217
Pictures: 'After Sunset,' 167; 'Afternoon,' 167; 'Before Sunrise,' 167; 'Brook

226

in May, The,' 158; 'Clay Cliffs, Block Island — Sunset,' 30; 'Coast of Maine (The) — East Wind,' 24; 'Dartmouth Moorlands,' 63, 177; 'Dawn' (2), 82, 83, 91; 'Dawn — Early Spring,' 152, 153; 'Drifting Clouds and Tumbling Sea,' 167; 'Dutch Boats in a Breeze,' 48; 'Eagle Lake, Morning Mist,' 30; 'East Wind,' 167; 'Evening,' 82; 'Evening Light,' 30; 'First Leaves,' 150; 'Green Mountain from Otter Creek,' 30; 'Gunning Rock — Narragansett Pier,' 24; 'Harvest in Normandy,' 48; 'Harvest Time in Normandy,' 46; 'Haystack, The,' 69; 'Light Northeast Wind, A,' 167; 'Man with the Glove' (copy), 49; 'May,' 158; 'Meadows of Conway, The,' 30; 'Misty Morning, A,' 167; 'Moonlight,' 167; 'Newport at Night,' 66; 'Moonlit Sea,' 167; 'Night — New England,' 158; 'Northeaster, A,' 167; 'October Fields,' 91; 'Northwest Wind Making Up,' 167; 'Rising Moon, The,' 77, 78; 'River Maas, The,' 48; 'River Maas at Dordrecht, The,' 90; 'Salt Marsh (A) — December,' 90; 'Sea-Evening, The,' 167; 'Sea Moods,' 91, 167, 189; 'Sea-Night, The,' 167; 'Sea Phases,' see 'Sea Moods'; 'Shift of Wind from East to Northwest,' 167; 'Spring Morning,' 161; 'Springtime,' 82–84; 'Surf, South-East Point,' 30; 'Twilight,' 91; 'Twilight Seas,' 168; 'White Hills from Jefferson, The,' 30; 'Windmills,' 48; 'Winter,' 82

Tryon, Watson, brother of Anson, 8

Tryons, the, 8

Tryontown, 10

Turner, Joseph M. W., 36; and Tryon, 51 55; biographies of, 52; his fondness for fishing, 130

Twachtman, artist, 90

Twain, Mark. See Clemens, Samuel L.

Twichell, Rev. Dr. Joseph H., 27, 28

Vollon, the pictures of, 51

Wadsworth, Daniel, 19

Wadsworth Athenæum, Hartford, 19

Walker, Horatio, artist, 75

Warner, Charles Dudley, 27

Watts, George Frederick, artist, 95

Weir, artist, 90

Weirs, the, 36

West, Benjamin, portrait of, 19

West, Capt., of Padanaram, 64

Whaling industry, 59, 60

Wheeler, William R., portrait painter, 31

Whistler, James McNeill, 36, 80, 81, 84, 90; letters of, 39–41; quoted, 138, 215

Whiting, Dr. F., owner of 'Night — New England,' 158

Williams, George Alfred, artist, 66, 146; letters of Tryon to, 82, 156, 167

Williams, Mary R., assistant of Tryon in Smith College Art School, 98

Woolf, Albert, quoted, 171

Wyant, Alexander H., artist, 24, 80, 120

Yale, Dr. Leroy M., physician and etcher, 117, 147

THE PANTHEON AT NIGHT, PARIS

THE WEIR, MONCHAUX

PARIS, EVENING

NOTRE DAME

CERNAY LA VILLE

VENICE

FRENCH VILLAGE, EVENING

GLASTONBURY MEADOWS

EVENING, NEW BEDFORD HARBOR

MOONRISE, NEAR THE SHORE

SELF PORTRAIT

EARLY SPRING

SALT MARSHES, DECEMBER

SCENE AT NEW BEDFORD

DAWN

OCTOBER FIELDS

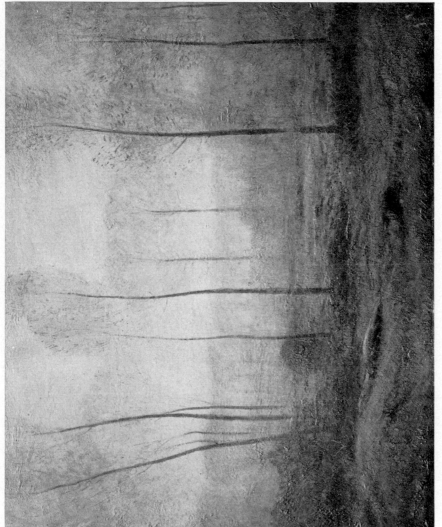

TWILIGHT, MAY

PENCIL DRAWING OF TREES

SPRINGTIME

THE SEA BEFORE SUNRISE

PENCIL STUDY FOR A PAINTING

AUTUMN, NEW ENGLAND

NOVEMBER MORNING

NOVEMBER

MAY MORNING

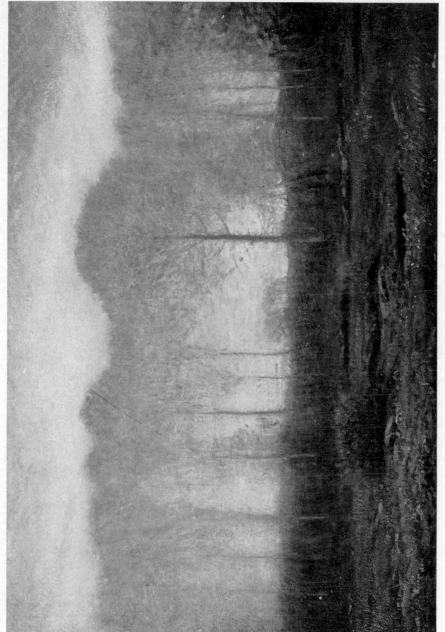

TWILIGHT, EARLY SPRING

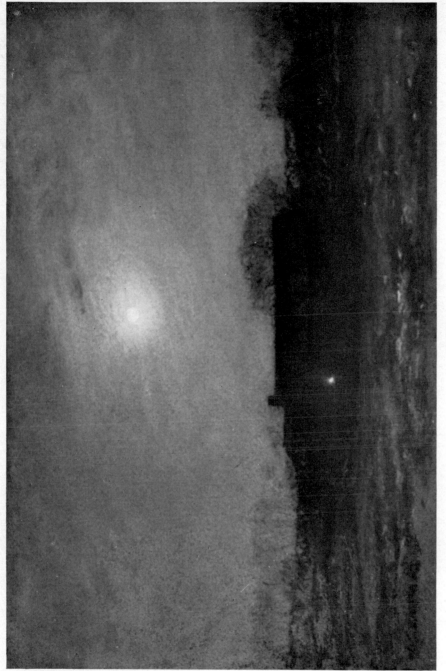

NIGHT

EVENING, LOOKING EAST

OCTOBER MORNING

NOVEMBER EVENING
The artist's last picture

NIGHT, NEW ENGLAND